FIVE WEEKS IN NOVEMBER

Five Weeks in November

A Brief Commentary on the Florida Election Results

Richard S. Weiss

Writer's Showcase
San Jose New York Lincoln Shanghai

Five Weeks in November
A Brief Commentary on the Florida Election Results

Writer's Showcase
an imprint of iUniverse.com, Inc.

For information address:
iUniverse.com, Inc.
5220 S 16th, Ste. 200
Lincoln, NE 68512
www.iuniverse.com

ISBN: 0-595-19966-6

Printed in the United States of America

Contents

Epigraph vii

INTRODUCTION ix

1. THE LOTTERY 1

2. CHASER AND CHASEE 8

3. THE POPULAR VOTE AND THE ELECTORAL COLLEGE ..13

4. THE STEALING OF THE ELECTION 20

5. THE MILITARY VOTE 30

6. THE CONCESSION 34

7. THE REVOTE 36

8. THE RECOUNT 41

9. DISENFRANCHISED 45

10. THE TEST OF DEMOCRACY 51

11. PARTISANSHIP 56

12. THE OPPORTUNITY OF A LIFETIME 61

13. THE FLORIDA SUPREME COURT 67

14. THE SUPREME COURT 70

15. CLOSURE 80

16. SECOND CHANCE 101

Epigraph

A unique analysis of how Al Gore chose a course of action in the post-Florida election that sealed his ultimate downfall

INTRODUCTION

They say that passion is dead. As the world becomes more technologically oriented, they say the old values have died or are dying. True love, courtship, and family—these are all things that are dying or soon will be dead.

Love and courtship are being trivialized, not only by premarital sex but also by the casual attitude of teenagers toward sex. The ease with which young people go into drugs and other illicit matters is alarming.

Perhaps the above is true. I am not really sure. However, if we want to focus on one of these matters, I can resoundingly say that those naysayers are definitely wrong. I find passion to be very much alive and the fervor and conviction of one's beliefs to be amazingly important by many people; especially people that you might not have thought could manifest such emotions and beliefs.

This new-found awakening of passion, this catalyst of fervent beliefs, came to the forefront with the 2000 presidential election.

More specifically, the election itself could have been placed in the category of the same ho-hum "business as usual" occurrence that marks most elections, even presidential elections. However, it was the almost unique happening in Florida that catalyzed a nation into the tremendous interest and passion that gripped the United States from the beginning of the result of the election on election day for five full weeks until the final court decision on December 12th by the Supreme Court that essentially determined the final outcome of the election.

As high as the emotions ran during the uncertainty in Florida, the flaming passion exhibited during this time by the majority of the country was quickly extinguished after the final and controlling

Supreme Court decision. (Perhaps this means that passion and interest in a cause or in an idea does not have the staying power that it once had, but this might be a topic for another time.)

What I further found, and what is the basis for prompting me to write this book, is the fact that with the passion that the election created, there was a corresponding element of irrationality that went with it. Perhaps part of the definition of passion is that of unpredictability, irrationality, or just plain stupidity that all becomes elements of passion. Nevertheless, I was personally appalled at the degree and extent to which this irrationality manifested itself. Not only was this irrationality found in practically everybody who voiced an opinion, but this blatant retreat from logic also extended to the people in charge—the talking heads, if you will, of television and the media who we rely upon to give us our news and second-hand guidance.

In broadcast journalism, the public and national forum for news announcers, impartiality is crucial. One will not get anywhere if their voice and mannerisms reflect the origins of their background. Practically all announcers and public figures will strive to lose their southern, western, or Boston accent to mask their regional origins when they are performing their job.

By the same token, a news announcer must deliver his or her news and information without portraying personal political, economic, ethnic or religious views.

While it might be acceptable for sports announcers to favor their home teams and religious leaders to extol the wonders of God, this bias does not extend to the newscasters delivering the national news.

One would hope that in today's world, most enlightened people have views that are not contrary to what we (mostly) accept as the right position to take in various matters. The term "political correctness" says it all with respect to this. Therefore, an announcer who might still harbor personal views that some would think are racist or discriminatory can function very well in today's world, so long as those views remain hidden. I believe to a great extent that the news announcers of the world have mastered this art quite handsomely.

I am sure that not every single newscaster and announcer is politically perfect. Yet we, as the consumers, have little trouble listening to a professional newscaster and hearing what he says without a hint of that person's private views, views we might find repugnant if we knew what they were.

Even most public figures that one might feel are actually biased against a certain race or ethnic class, national figures that are not politically correct, still do not come out and blatantly extol views that would generally alienate them from the populace at large.

Patrick Buchanan ran for President, and he debated Alan Dershowitz several times as Mr. Dershowitz suggested that some of the statements and actions of Mr. Buchanan implied his prejudice against the Jewish populace. Mr. Buchanan vehemently denied this and it became a cat-and-mouse game when Mr. Buchanan was called to task for these supposed views. Mr. Buchanan could rationalize all of his statements and positions, no matter how tortuously he had to bend logic to do it.

Nevertheless, even if Mr. Buchanan has prejudices which are not politically correct or socially acceptable, he has conducted himself so that his statements in those areas are ambiguous at best, and it is left to the insightful receiver of his message to decide exactly whether he was in fact railing against a certain ethnic group, or whether his remarks were neutral. This deceptiveness becomes an art in and of itself.

Also true is that there exists a small segment of people who are less quixotic in their non-political assessment of certain situations. These people actually want to be politically incorrect and have incendiary views because this is what their platform and their following demand. They actually gain their political base from like thinking people, albeit and hopefully in the minority, who are readily willing to adopt their radical views. Louis Farrakhan and Randy Metzger come to mind as national figures who have minority views but who are very willing and happy to stand by their views in order to attract like-thinking people to their causes.

Moving to the 2000 Presidential election, I was absolutely appalled at the fact that for the most part, from the common man up to and including members of the Supreme Court, virtually no person who had any knowledge or interest in the election itself could express a view, listen to the facts, or rationally discuss it without couching any of their statements, views, and arguments to the political side with which they were aligned.

This is not to say that the average run-of-the-mill American citizen, or for that matter a national announcer, is afraid or ashamed to allow his political affiliation to permeate his thinking or his arguments when he discusses them. Someone such as Geraldo Rivera makes no bones about his political affiliation.

Indeed, all elected officials who are a stated Republican or Democrat are obviously going to couch their arguments framed by their respective political philosophies.

However, I believe this goes only so far. It is true that there are many votes in the Congress and state legislatures that are purely partisan in nature. This is done for two distinct reasons. First, the person's beliefs adhere to and are swayed by the political line of his party. This makes sense because this particular person chose to be called either a Republican or a Democrat because he did agree, for the most part, with the philosophy of that party. Second, there may be a completely partisan vote because of the way politics work and in various situations, the elected official is expected to vote "the party line."

However, when the issue at hand, the tie vote, was created by the extraordinary election results in Florida, it did not necessarily have to be that each and every person who talked about this matter and wanted to express an opinion, had to be absolutely and undeniably governed by partisan comments, that in my opinion, went greatly beyond the logic of the whole situation. Nor did virtually each and every person who ever uttered an opinion on this matter have to be so wholly or totally governed by the partisan line that the opinions never rose to independent thinking because of the iron grip that partisanship seems to have exerted in this issue.

I certainly did not hear each and every opinion proffered by every talk show host and newscaster. Nevertheless, I did hear enough of the opinions at different stages of the election, from election night to the time that each talk show employed half of a dozen analysts to wait for the final decision of the Supreme Court at 10:00 P.M. on December 12, 2000.

Even as that decision was being read, the partisanship and emotions were as strong as ever. The Democrats immediately began lamenting that this was the most tragic decision they had ever encountered in their political careers, and the Republicans were lauding the decision as a brilliant one rendered by the highest court in the land.

I believe the election itself was a fascinating convergence of politics, statistics, strategy, and luck that needs an independent voice to put things into perspective.

In contemplating writing this brief monologue, I thought that many people far more qualified than I will certainly write such an analysis, and indeed I am sure that over the years this will certainly happen. However, I also began to think that perhaps many great minds would not quite be able to write such an analysis because of the very partisanship to which they most likely adhere and as a result obviously could not render an even-handed assessment of the situation.

Therefore, it seems it is left to the smattering of people out there who can be non-partisan to write an analysis that will be even-handed and will not betray the political leanings of the author.

I would like to think that I fall into this category. Hopefully, the following chapters, many (or most) which will be no more than a restatement of basic concepts the reader already knows, will be written in a manner that does not betray my political affiliation. Only in this way can an analysis be made that will be acceptable and logical to parties on both sides of the issue.

I also feel that for die-hard Republicans and Democrats, the issue will never be settled for them. There will always be undercurrents of animosity and distrust on the part of rabid Republicans and Democrats.

On this point, I believe that there actually is an answer to this election, perhaps Solomonic in stature, and if it can be approached open-mindedly, that should at least settle, and to some extent, mollify the people who still might be upset over the results of the election. After all, we will have four years of George W. Bush, and after that, there will be a dogfight as to whether Mr. Bush gets another four years, Mr. Gore is able to unseat him, or some other political player will come upon the stage.

When the time for the next national election comes, I am sure the political maelstrom created by this election will rise again, and there will be the same strident and unswerving arguments and pig-headed positions that will divide down party lines. I would like to think that my analysis and explanation of the final Supreme Court decision will (or can) explain and also legitimatize the final decision. My analysis, while not the ultimate answer and panacea for the Democrats, should be accepted as the "shot" that Al Gore took, and satisfy everyone that everybody gave it their best try, perhaps had a course of action that would secure them victory, and in the case of the Democrats, came back second best. One cannot ask for more.

1

THE LOTTERY

As happens every four years, the country has been witness to the spectacle of the run for the Presidency, essentially by two major parties, the Republican and Democratic. In today's sophisticated age, the American populous is sophisticated enough to generally understand that we have a two party system, that the two party system has basic differences in philosophy, and that these differences manifest themselves in the different ideas and policies for which each candidate stands.

Armed with this knowledge, the candidates hit the campaign trail to bring their policies to the people to persuade and cement the people who agree with their policies, and more importantly, attempt to persuade, convince, charm and cajole both the people on the other side, and more importantly, the people "on the fence" politically to come over to their side of thinking. This is essentially the definition of campaigning.

Campaigning is done in a myriad of ways. For the Presidency, there are political ads, statements by the candidates themselves stating their position on each issue. There are party loyalists who campaign for their candidates by doing every thing from manning the phones to going out door-to-door trying to convince everybody they meet that their candidate is the better candidate.

Then there are strategies. Like it or not, there are certain areas and states that are known for their specific affiliations. Massachusetts has been Democratic since time began. There are other bastions of Democratic voters, and of course there are corresponding states that undeniably were going to go Republican in this campaign.

There was little question that Texas would vote Republican in the 2000 election if not for the voters' political views, then because George W. Bush was the candidate from Texas. While it might be surprising that Tennessee, Albert Gore's home state, did not "automatically" go for Mr. Gore (indeed, he lost the state), this was not that great a surprise, because this had happened in the past. Also, like it or not, the electoral votes presented from Tennessee were only 11 and not as big a prize as the votes of some of the more populated states.

Therefore, the strategies of the candidates naturally gravitated to the states that, on the whole, were "on the fence". While it was not 100% clear that a state was "on the fence," a state thought to be close might have gone decisively one way or the other in spite of the predictions of the pollsters, but nevertheless this meant that the strategy of the respective campaigns would be to target the states that they thought they were able to win, or win over, and devote much of their energies to trying to swing enough of the undecided votes so as to win the whole state.

In this election, there was little question in everybody's mind that the election was going to be extremely close. Everything might have broken badly for one of the candidates, and there could have been an unexpected landslide, or mini-landslide, but the general prediction was that the election would be very close.

This is not to say that each and every pollster could have predicted infallibly which way a state was going to go. However, as I previously stated, there were many states that were predestined to go for either one side or the other. Further, amongst all the states that were iffy, in predicting which way a state would go, the predictors might have been right or wrong on various states. If they were right on some and wrong on some, the net result would still be the same, which is of course what happened. The election was very close!

Obviously, Florida was such a state. Regardless of the intelligent or "correct" thinking as to which way Florida would go, the fact remains, bolstered by the actual results in Florida, that Florida certainly was on the fence.

Florida had approximately 6 million votes to contribute as its part of the popular vote of the whole country. From a statistical point of view, after all the campaigning and all the posturing was done and on November 7th Election Day, none of that mattered any more. Those who were going to vote voted, people had made up their minds, and their votes were cast.

After the smoke had cleared, the first count showed that Mr. Bush was several hundred votes ahead from over 6 million votes that were cast. There were still loose ends to be cleared up (overseas votes, military votes, etc.), but the essence of the vote was in. Mr. Bush's majority swelled at one point to 900 votes and, finally, the official margin of votes was approximately 573 votes in favor of Mr. Bush.

Again, this figure (not getting into all the recounts and chads and uncounted votes and votes rejected by the voting machines, to which I am not alluding in this section) essentially represented a tie.

Yes, I understand that it is not a tie because Mr. Bush prevailed by 500 votes. However, in our society, statistics are not only useful, but also govern many disciplines. In this case, if one were to factor in a situation where they said, "Well, we do want to know a true winner, but we feel that any marginal victory of less than a certain designated figure would be inconclusive (due to the very errors of chads, machine malfunctions, human error, and others), we should decide that if the margin of victory is small enough, then the election should be considered a tie."

This is a very logical approach to any election, and certainly could be implemented without going afoul of any laws or constitutional issues. The reason this is not done is very simple. The American public really has no complaint with the Democratic system and where one of the participants might win by the slimmest of margins, namely, one vote, no matter how many voters participate, this is an acceptable conclusion to an election.

The war cry is that the "will of the people has spoken." There is no question that the will of the people, by a simple majority, be it one vote in 100 million votes cast, it certainly is a majority (baring errors). Perhaps the American public is not so sophisticated that they have given thought to the fact that in such a close election the election itself should be declared a tie. The true will of the people is split virtually down the middle, and, therefore, the true will of the people is that they are equally divided between the candidates and not the fact that one of the candidates won by an insignificant margin.

The problem with this is that, as I have just said, the people themselves have no great problem with a party being elected by the slimmest of majorities. Second, if one were to declare statistical ties in elections that were this close, then we would have a problem in that we were seeking a person to fill a certain position, and the statistical tie does not render us a winner to step into the position sought. While the good news in accepting a statistical tie as a tie is that a winner would not be declared, it does certainly run afoul of the practicality of filling the position.

Also, where there was a statistical tie, if there were a revote, it would not be such a great idea to address the problem, because essentially you are dealing with the same population who were evenly split. The revote would only mirror the same individuals' opinions and create another statistical tie. If in fact there were a more decisive winner the second time around, this would probably be tainted and would not serve any meaningful purpose.

Therefore, on the one hand it is important that one understands just how even the vote was in Florida and should, for all intents and purposes, be considered equal. On the other hand, given the rules with which we went into the election, and indeed that we came out of the election with, it is also equally true that a majority, no matter how statistically insignificant it may be, is just that, and in most situations the party with the majority is called the winner.

The other side of the coin was, as many analysts had noted, even running to Justice Stevens on the Supreme Court, that we may never truly know who the actual winner in Florida was. However, if one accepts the premise of having a winner, no matter how insignificant the margin of difference, as long as we can say that one person received more votes than the other person, there is always going to be the inherent problem that we will never truly know who the actual precise majority vote-getter was in such a close election. We can always get a winner – the person whom we *THINK* received the most votes. But in reality, a super-close vote will only reflect the vagaries of human error. When it gets that close, we will never truly know for certain who received the most votes.

What then does all this have to do with the Lottery? The definition of a lottery is a winner chosen purely at chance. Everybody knows how it works. We all buy lottery tickets, the little ball bounces around, maybe gets blown out of the pile of balls by an air jet and that one number or several numbers come together to declare a winner.

Certainly no right-thinking person, except somebody who might be heavily imbued in lucky talismans, or who thinks he is the luckiest person alive, thinks that his chance is greater than any of the other participants in the lottery. Indeed, the concept of a lottery was thought to be so harmful to the fabric of a society that even the state itself was not allowed to run a lottery unless there was a special vote by the legislature to create a state-run lottery. For instance, this is exactly what happened in Massachusetts. We now have a highly successful lottery game, which was established about 28 or 29 years ago. However, prior to that time, a lottery as such was outlawed.

Accordingly, what I am suggesting is that the outcome of the vote in Florida was so close, so indistinguishable from the point of establishing an actual winner, that the actual candidate who emerged as the winner of the Florida vote was like a person who won the lottery.

Let us not forget that the essence of an election, and the corresponding campaigning that is done by the candidates, is to get that candidate's views and opinions and positions in front of the public. If the candidate does this and those views are clearly delineated to the voting public, the theory is,—which is the practicality of the situation,—that the majority of people who agree with such views will correspondingly vote for the candidate who espouses those same views. Again, this is all well and good because this is the reason for having elections.

The point is that while the whole country participated in the election, and the whole country was instrumental by its collective vote in determining the next president, it just worked out that the rest of the country votes were so equally divided that it left Florida to be the pivotal state. Coupling several concepts together, such as the concept of the electoral college (that is discussed in a future chapter) which essentially dictates that the electoral votes of a state go all or nothing to one candidate, the fact remains that because the vote was so close in Florida, the actual winner that emerged had no better credentials from the election than your run-of-the-mill lottery winner.

I am sure there are circumstances in which candidates are voted into office by some type of lottery. Occasionally, it is facetiously stated that the winner of such an election is really the loser of the election because he was unlucky to have won the position that held little interest for the rest of the participants.

Again, to put this argument into perspective, I am not trivializing the vote in Florida by saying that it was meaningless. Certainly a majority in resounding fashion, could have coalesced, and given a mandate for which candidate would have won the election. This, in fact, was the purpose of the election in the first place. But in analyzing what happened AFTER THE FACT, it turns out that because the population was so equally divided, then realistically, the person who was to win the vote, be it Mr. Gore or Mr. Bush, won, not because he was the resoundingly popular candidate, but because the giant roulette wheel in the sky was spun round and round and ended up landing on Mr. Bush's side, and not Mr. Gore's.

Again, this is not to say that in examining the results of the roulette wheel spin, it showed that Mr. Bush was the winner. He was not about to rescind this decision because of the statistical insignificance of it; by the same token, he is not going to trumpet how he was the overwhelming victor in the 2000 presidential election! (Let us not forget that he lost the total popular vote of all the 50 states by a hefty 200,000 to 300,000 votes).

In conclusion, the point of this chapter is not to bemoan the fact that Mr. Gore was not chosen to lead the country, or that Mr. Bush was the overwhelmingly popular choice of the American public. Given the fallibility of counting 6 million votes precisely correct, as Justice Stevens noted in his dissent from the Supreme Court decision (that we may never know who the actual winner in Florida was), I am suggesting that the person who earned the right to call himself the winner of the Florida vote was the man who won the Florida lottery, not the Florida election!

2

CHASER AND CHASEE

In light of the Florida results, it is clear that the voting public was virtu-ally evenly split between the two candidates. While it is true that if either party were to get his post election argument accepted and have certain portions of the votes reexamined, such as the block of votes in Broward and Dade Counties that appeared to be favorable to Mr. Gore, have certain other votes and more of the military votes allowed to be included in the count, that the general thought was that they would be more beneficial to Mr. Bush, this would still have rendered a STATISTI-CAL tie. This is so because even if the count for one candidate became a several thousand-vote majority for one candidate, we would still be in a statistical tie, given the enormous base of six million votes that were cast in total for both candidates.

Therefore, to fully understand the results of the vote and the manifestation of those results, one should think of a giant roulette wheel spinning around and the landing of the little ball either on red or black, each color being designated as the respective color of each candidate. As random as the roulette wheel is, this is as random as finding either Mr. Bush or Mr. Gore prevailed in the election (given the even split of the votes).

This is not to say that prior to the Florida vote, the vote was going to be that way.Again, both candidates campaigned vigorously in Florida and the polls might have indicated either candidate to have a significant (statistical) edge.Even in considering the roulette concept of who won, this concept would only be applicable if indeed the vote was going to be as close as it was.

However, the vote WAS that close, and we are back to our roulette wheel concept.

I am suggesting that when the voting process began and the voters cast their votes (and, in this case, because of the even split of the vote), it was as if a giant roulette wheel spun around and around and ended on either Mr. Bush or Mr. Gore as the victor. The vote WAS so close that it would be pure luck whether Mr. Gore or Mr. Bush would have had such a slight lead after all the votes had been tallied.

The point is that when the roulette wheel did stop and a "winner" was clearly established, the new rules of the game were set up.

The candidates now had to accept their new roles as the "Chaser" and "Chasee."

This seemingly random occurrence had more than an incidental effect on the participants. The effect, of course, was the fact that we had both a WINNER AND LOSER, regardless of the insignificance of the differential, and regardless of the fact that perhaps the malfunction of one mechanical counting machine (independent of even all the fights about partial indentations and chads and hanging chads) that did not even come to the attention of any of the officials monitoring the counting, would have been able to alter the true vote enough to establish a "winner", regardless of, and in spite of, the other six million votes.

This is the problem in a very close election, and a statistically significant winner. In other words, a significantly statistical winner could rely on the actual votes cast and rise above and blunt any arguments that he might have won because of such a malfunction or such a mix-up in the counting of the votes. A decisive winner relies on the overwhelming majority of votes to essentially silence his opponents. From a statistical point of view, when one tries to interject malfunctions and misunderstandings and even petty fraud into something that is deemed statistically significant, then the significance of the statistics itself renders the decision much more likely to be accurate. When the finding is statistically insignificant, as it was in this election, not only is the actual winner statistically insignificant, but the will of the people is rendered almost moot when and if post election challenges are begun. Much to the horror of the leader and the delight of the loser, if enough irregularities are uncovered, the outcome of the election might be altered.

Accordingly, whether random or not, the election established both a winner and a loser.

Obviously, the significance of having a winner and a loser cannot be underestimated. That was the objective of the election itself, and to a limited extent, that objective was satisfied because a winner was established (regardless of the fact that it only might have been temporary).

Therefore, within the context of the election, a winner emerged from the election. However, in the context of how close it was, again an after-fact analysis, the winner, the person who emerged with more votes could be considered enormously lucky to have done that, and the person who received the fewer votes became incredibly unlucky in this respect.

The outcome of the election also established who the frontrunner was going to be, (the chasee if you will) and who the person who was to be the chaser would be. In determining these roles, it did not matter what the winning margin was. The fact is that the roles were determined and each candidate had to accept the obligations that being the winner or the loser carried with it. This also obviously set the rules and the agenda for each candidate.

There are things in our language that are called idioms, wise sayings, and quotable quotes. One of the more popular quotes connected with law is, "possession is nine-tenths of the law." What this means is that right or wrong, regardless who might be the true owner of an object, the person who winds up with possession of that object has a tremendous advantage over the other party, whether or not that party has a legitimate claim to the item.

I have found this concept to be quite accurate in document disputes. When there is a dispute as to the validity of a document, whether there has been a deed to a property given and fraud alleged, or if there has been a written contract between the parties and one of the parties then claims that the contract was invalid because there had been a misprinting of one of the terms of the contract, the party trying to alter the written document is at an enormous disadvantage. It is not necessarily impossible to overcome, but the work is cut out for the party challenging the contract as written. In the case of the 2000 Presidential election, the party which garnered fewer votes, no matter how many fewer, now had the enormous task of trying to turn that situation around. That party had the formidable task of attempting to rewrite the results to become winner of the election!

Obviously, the task of the chaser fell to Mr. Gore. No matter how unfair these few votes that made Mr. Bush the leader became, the enormous task of trying to overturn or change the results, if you will, by recounting or any other of the methods legally available to Mr. Gore, was the rather enormous task with which Mr. Gore was faced.

One might say that there was a corresponding obligation or task that fell upon the chasee, in this case Mr. Bush, in that it may not have been necessarily the right thing for him to stand by and do nothing while Mr. Gore pulled out any and all stops and strategies to do what he thought he had to do to change the election results. There was no prohibition against Mr. Bush doing equally as much to attempt to insure and protect his lead. In fact, Mr. Bush did employ both ends of the strategy spectrum. Where he had to, Mr. Bush brought lawsuits and attempted to have certain votes counted and certain votes excluded. By and large, he also did what the age-old homily suggests: he stood perhaps by, "took a wait and see position" watched to see if Mr. Gore, the person who only had one-tenth of the law on his side, was able to overturn the original results of the election.

3

THE POPULAR VOTE AND THE ELECTORAL COLLEGE

As most people know, the way a President is elected is governed by the rules of and in conjunction with the Electoral College. The Electoral College is a somewhat antiquated procedure with which the common man is somewhat uneasy, but not so uneasy that he seriously attempts to do anything about it.

Of course, when we have to implement the Electoral College, that is, when we are electing a president, the stilted procedure of the Electoral College weighs on people far more significantly. Nevertheless, as something like this only arises periodically, the brouhaha dies down after the Electoral College and its procedure is implemented, only to be shoved aside until the next time that we need it, in the next presidential election in four years.

Such was the case with our previous Presidential Election. This time, however, the Electoral College took center stage due to several factors, one being the closeness of the Florida election and secondly, the fact that Mr. Bush had a significantly lower popular vote than the second place finisher, Mr. Gore.

What is the Electoral College? It exists because the original founding fathers created a system that is similar to the House of Representatives and Senate in our American judiciary. The Electoral College is controversial because it does not absolutely mirror the popular vote. The Electoral College awards all its electors (votes) to the absolute winner of the popular vote of a single state, no matter how slim the margin. This system allows the very real possibility that a candidate who has not gained a majority of the popular vote may very well garner the majority of the electoral votes, thus winning the election.

This system is really a mirror and combination of how our arms of Congress work. One could say that the arms of Congress are made in an almost perfect way, from a check and balance point of view. Simply by creating a Senate and a House of Representatives, our founding fathers were able to serve the needs of nothing less than the diverse needs of a whole country. When one considers the size of the United States, if it were not obvious at first, one should now recognize that there is going to be a wide divergence in the makeup of the population from state to state.

This is so because certain states develop certain collective needs. This phenomenon occurs for several different reasons: first, a region might be populated by an ethnic group which dictates its own customs and needs; a region close to the sea dictates a predominately seafaring environment; other regions may be blessed with fertile land to accomplish a successful agricultural economy; and yet other states might have their own unique offerings.

Accordingly, with each state's physical makeup will come a corresponding makeup of its population. The most obvious aspect of the population, not counting the ethnicity that each population may reflect, is both the size of the population and the ratios of concentration of the population in cities and in the countryside. What all this means is that different states have vastly different needs and points of view.

One can say that all of these considerations mirror the manifestation of peopling the House and the Senate.

In a masterful stroke, the founding fathers were able to find a way to appease both the heavily populated states as well as the more rural states. This was done by the requirements for the Senate and the House of Representatives. At first blush, the founding fathers stated that each state should have the right to contribute two Senators to a national body so that each state would be equally represented among all of their sister states. This, of course, is the makeup of the Senate. Thereafter, the founding fathers were able to appease the more heavily populated states and with it their argument that they should have more say in national matters because they contribute more people to the United States as a whole. These more populated states were satisfied by having a House of Representatives. Presently we have states that due to their sparse populations, contribute as few as one person to the House of Representatives, Idaho for example, has one Representative, while California presently contributes 52 members to the House of Representatives. One could say that the founding fathers masterfully appeased all interests to bind the individual states into a national body.

With respect to the national vote for President, the founding fathers foresaw the following problem, that being the more heavily populated areas would dominate the choosing of a candidate. They decided that the best solution, without getting too complicated, would be to set up a system similar to the House of Representatives. Therefore, the Electoral College contributes Electors to the ultimate voting of the President in proportion to their population. The founding fathers felt that it was not necessary to have a corresponding and perhaps competing system like the Senate, but that each state would have an absolute right to have a proportionate say in the national election according to its status as a state. This also seems wise because while Senators and Congressmen might have far more time to hash out and debate national issues, the founding fathers recognized the fact that they needed a more or less immediate system to address the election of a President.

Therefore, the Electoral College was created then and presently exists now. Due to the makeup of the Electoral College, and the fact that the Constitution cannot be changed unless there is a three-fourths vote of all the states, it would seem realistic that the Electoral College will not be abolished in the foreseeable future unless something significant and unexpected occurs so that even the smallest states, which the Electoral College system seems to favor, suggest that the Electoral College is not meeting the needs of modern America and must be changed.

The fact is that what we witnessed in the Florida election will probably never be witnessed again in our lifetimes. The factors that caused the focus of attention on Florida were so unique that one could reasonably predict that something like this will never happen again in the foreseeable future.

Not only did the Florida vote have an amazing number of factors come together at very long odds, but the system of the Electoral College, while it perhaps did come under severe criticism, easily withstood the crisis of Florida (if one wants to call it a crisis). If it could withstand the 2000 Presidential Election, there will probably not be enough ground swell to have it changed in the future.

Accordingly, in dealing with the Electoral College, the main and most significant thing that can occur of any merit is the fact that it is possible that a person can be elected President without having the majority of the popular vote. Basically, this can occur when certain states vote almost by landslide proportions for one candidate, which bolsters that candidate's popular vote, but in other states, the votes are so close that the winning candidate has almost an insignificant majority. However, as is also mentioned throughout this book, regardless of the insignificance of the majority, if a majority is established, then that party is the winner of that state and thus wins ALL the electoral votes. Obviously, this creates a somewhat disproportionate allocation of electoral votes versus popular votes, but this is the manifestation of the Electoral College.

The fact has been pointed out many times by more of the knowledgeable and sensible commentators in this matter that, regardless of what the Electoral College is or is not, it certainly was in place at the time this election occurred, namely November 7th of 2000. There is an age-old understanding that fair play demands that the parties adhere to the rules that originally existed when the game (election) began. When this game began to elect a President, the Electoral College was in place, and certainly both participants were well aware of the rules of the game. Therefore, one can say that it was inevitable that if the person with the smaller popular vote became President, it was easy enough for the loser (but victor in popular vote) if grossly misdirected, to declare that, yes, he had lost the electoral vote but had won the popular vote! Again, for either candidate to bring this up in order to gain the sympathy of the country and try to muddy the waters of popular opinion does a disservice to his own credibility. That is why, I believe, Mr. Gore did not dwell on this fact; but he did let his supporters run rampant on the subject.

Mr. Gore did not dwell on the fact that he was the popular winner, but it certainly was brought up often enough by his team and the American public was not allowed to forget it. Those who demand honesty and straightforwardness from their candidates, without specious reasoning, should have become annoyed or even enraged by references to the unfairness of the popular vote versus the electoral vote.

The 2000 election did not set a precedent. We have had several candidates get into office who had not received the majority of the popular vote. In 1876, Rutherford B. Hayes did not receive the popular vote, and the election of 1820 saw Andrew Jackson denied the Presidency although he received the popular vote. While it is true that the candidates who were elected without the popular vote usually did not distinguish themselves, the fact remains that they did assume office and no tragic or catastrophic things occurred during their Presidencies.

One should also understand that given the nature of the Electoral College versus the popular vote, and given the fact that if a scenario were created like that in Florida (where in the vote was so close that it threw the process into turmoil, and the state became the pivotal state), it would declare the ultimate Presidential winner. Logically then, there had to exist a situation in which there was a 50/50 chance that the winner of Florida (and the then to be crowned President) might very well be the candidate with fewer popular votes.

To understand this, one must realize that unless each and every other state in the Union has a razor thin or almost minuscule majority determining the Presidential winner, if all the votes from all the other 49 states were tallied there had to be one of the two candidates with the lead in the popular vote. The lead could have been less than the two or three hundred thousand votes that actually manifested themselves, or it could have been more. Again, the votes would have been determined in the manner that I have stated, where, in some states, the candidate who won the state won it by such a significant majority that it tilted the evenness of the vote where another candidate might have won another state by such a slim majority that the actual votes were virtually even.

Therefore, it did not matter when one was going to unscramble the closeness of the Florida election, that one of the candidates would have a popular vote lead on the other candidate. Obviously, we all know that in this case, it was Mr. Gore who emerged with the leading popular vote. To my mind, this is similar to the lottery chapter in which I wrote that it just happened to work out that Mr. Gore amassed more of the popular vote than Mr. Bush.

Because of the role that Florida played, we had the results of a vote that was so close that no winner (i.e., a party that actually had the absolute majority of the votes) could be realistically determined with any degree of confidence. We then would experience what ultimately occurred: a series of challenges and other safeguards were undertaken by both sides to allow each to exhaust its respective legal remedies. When the ultimate winner was declared, the decision was then molded into an acceptable legal pronouncement in conjunction with the total rulings of the court. Because this would only occur if the actual Florida vote were so close as to be impossible to determine a winner from either side, it stands to reason that one of the parties was going to be leading in the popular vote and the other party would have to be second. Since we now shift our attention to the fact that both parties were so close that it stands to reason that there was a 50/50 chance that the winner of Florida, who would ultimately be declared the next President, could very well have had less of the popular vote.

This, in fact, occurred because Mr. Bush won and Mr. Gore didn't. Had Mr. Gore won, there would have been a better alignment of the electoral votes and the popular votes, but there still would have been the same razor thin results that determined that Mr. Gore was the winner over Mr. Bush. The irony still would be there, but at least the winner of the electoral votes would have matched the winner of the popular votes.

4

THE STEALING OF THE ELECTION

As soon as it became obvious what was happening with the election results in Florida, it became equally clear to the respective camps that things were going to happen. For the most part, these "things" manifested themselves in various lawsuits in order to first ascertain a recount, and secondarily to define exactly what should occur in areas where the recount itself was not obvious. This second area of concern has to do with the now extremely well known chads, hanging chads, dimpled votes that may or may not be counted, butterfly votes that were confusing and perhaps did not meet constitutional muster and should be redone, talk of an actual re-voting in Florida, and many other scenarios that became more bizarre as the parties contemplated putting them into use.

I have alluded several times in this book to the fact that the recount in the year 2000 was far more sophisticated than in times past. Correspondingly, there would be subtle differences in what was to transpire, given the fact that a recount in the year 2000 would not be subject to the horrors of election results in years past. The fact remained that there was no question that things were going to happen and things would be done by both sides in an attempt to fully protect their rights with respect to the ultimate outcome of the presidential election.

With the phenomenon of the Florida vote came the respective concerns of each camp. First, each camp was explicitly defined by whether it was the leader or the chaser. While in other parts of this book I have delineated my view that given the actual results of the Florida election, it was virtually random whether Mr. Bush or Mr. Gore would emerge as the slight absolute leader or slight absolute chaser with respect to the election results. Nevertheless, whoever was to be the leader and chaser, this clearly defined the respective roles of each camp.

One might think that in the post election hubbub it would only be left to the chaser to take all the action and make all the moves in order to attempt to thwart and reverse the election results so that he would be the ultimate winner.

However, the situation was hardly as simple as that, and it was obvious that with these results, neither party was easily in a secure position. This could only mean that both parties had to make great efforts and take great precautions in formulating their game plans. For Mr. Gore, it was obvious that he had to use aggressive tactics in order to "make things happen" in the hope of spurring to some type of recount that would make him the leader. Mr. Bush had to examine the situation, ensure that Mr. Gore did not overstep his bounds, and perhaps try to short circuit any such measure that Mr. Bush found improper. This policing would have to be done by rulings of the courts.

To me, it was at this point that the real passion of America manifested itself. I was absolutely amazed at the fervor and zeal that was exhibited by the common people of America on both ends of the political spectrum. Each political faction and each votary either somewhat understood the process or was willing to go along with his more educated brethren in voicing his political opinion and attempting to enforce their respective situations. The Democrats sloughed off (and rightly so) any notion of impropriety in attempting to have a recount, and the Republicans kept harping on the fact that Mr. Bush actually won the election. After all, the votes came out at first that Mr. Bush was a 170-vote winner, thereafter a 900-vote winner, and finally settling on a 572-vote winner.

One of the very first things that prompted me to write this book was the subsequent rhetoric by each side and the blatant disregard for logic and the application of law in the recount chase.

While I believe that the misinformation and constant perversion of facts can be forgiven or even overlooked by people who are not political students, I am absolutely appalled at the same misinformation, and partisan arguments promulgated by the parties who were supposedly the leaders of each respective party and the parties whose voice would be or should have been relied upon by its followers of that party to state their position kept being reiterated over and over again. It is no wonder that virtually every Democrat and Republican spouted his party's ridiculous line, because I found that not one political analyst was able to comment on the situation in a neutral and fair manner. I found it comical that virtually each and every analyst could easily be identified as a Republican or a Democrat by the way he spoke and the logic that he attempted to use to bolster his political position.

As Mr. Gore relentlessly pursued his avenues in courts, the Republican mantra became "How many times does George Bush have to win?" He won the original vote and he won two recounts. Just how many times did he need to win, and why are the Democrats doing this? It is just a futile attempt to steal the election.

Let us examine exactly what was happening in Florida, and who, if anybody, was attempting to steal the election.

If most people did not understand, then they certainly understand now that after an election, there are rather extensive provisions for a recount. Not only can the recount process begin, but there are obvious situations where one side or another might go into court either for clarification of some rule, or to institute some procedure, such as the recount.

For instance, recounts are only triggered by the closeness of the vote. Obviously, one can have a sore loser who garners thirty percent of the vote, and just to show his displeasure and to irritate everyone within earshot, demands his "constitutional right" to a recount, if in fact a recount can always be demanded. Therefore, there are guidelines that will determine when a recount should kick in.

Like everything else in a situation such as this, the guidelines themselves may become blurry for a variety of reasons, perhaps irregularity of voting practices, defectiveness of machines, improperly managed voting stations, or many other things too innumerable to mention. These might suggest to the party seeking a recount that perhaps he is entitled to a recount, even if it is not quite to the letter of the law that he should be allowed to have one.

This is no more than what Mr. Gore attempted to do when he began his quest to try to overturn the election results.

Analyzing the situation from the Republican perspective one has the talking heads decrying the tactics of the Democrats. But did or do the Republicans have any right to criticize the Democrats for only exercising their legal right as guaranteed by the laws of both Florida and the United States?

What was not said—was not said loudly enough by the Democrats – was that each and every thing they did with respect to the courts was absolutely legal, and far more importantly, absolutely allowed and condoned by the courts. Why is this so? For the very simple and logical reason that if it were improper, the courts would have shut Mr. Gore down by just saying "No, you cannot do this." In other words, in our society, the courts are the final arbiters of what is right and wrong or what is legal and illegal. In this situation, the Democrats are not fighting at the polling place, trying to out-scream their Republican counterparts that they have the right to do this or that, or attempting to flex their muscles and actually intimidate any people who would stand in their way to stop the Democrats from doing whatever they thought they should do to overturn the election results. This was far from being the case.

The Democrats may very well have conceived or concocted some situation they felt could gain them a legal foothold or advantage in this skirmish. They then went into court and attempted to back up their position with the blessing of the court. Again, it cannot be emphasized too much that at that point in time, the combatants were right in the arena where a final decision must be made and that would be by the courts themselves. If what the Democrats were trying to do were deemed improper or illegal, the courts very simply would have stated that it was improper and would have terminated all further advancements in that area.

This is exactly what happened regarding the final determinations, first by the Florida Supreme Court and ultimately by the U.S. Supreme Court. In other words, while the decision has been greatly criticized, and in some situations wrongly condemned as inimical to the well-being of the country, the Supreme Court did render a decision at 10:00 on December 12, 2000 that ultimately had the absolute effect of stopping all further inquiries into the election (i.e., stopping all recounts) and de-facto declaring that Mr. Bush was the winner by dint of the fact that the recounts could not go forward because they were being conducted in an unconstitutional manner.

It cannot be denied that the proof of the pudding in this case is that each and every thing that Mr. Gore did up to that point had actually been given the blessing of the court. I am not saying that the blessing of the court was the agreement that whatever Mr. Gore was asking to be done was the correct thing or that the court encouraged him to do it, but I mean that the courts said, "Yes, you have the legal right to do this thing you are asking us for permission to do."

Accordingly, I found it incredibly appalling that at that time, the Republicans were condemning Mr. Gore's quest to protect his legal rights and to maintain his rights in his attempt to obtain a recount, thus putting the election on hold.

While each of us with a passing interest in listening to the political analysts talk, but without the time to hear each and every person on television who was allowed to espouse an opinion, I found the remarks of James Baker for the Republicans especially irresponsible and detrimental to the process that was going on, and therefore ultimately to the Democratic process as being manifested by the recount. Mr. Baker seemed to be appealing almost on a moral or evangelical level that the actions of Mr. Gore were wrong and harmful to the country. As usual, his analysis and comments flew in the face of what was allowed, permissible, and actually condoned by the courts.

Another theme that constantly runs through this book is the fact that while parties on both sides of the issue were entitled to their respective opinions and actions, and while each side's opinions appeared to be excruciatingly partisan, the fact remains that the side espousing the correct legal position to the question in hand becomes the correct entity at that point in time, regardless whether their position is fueled solely upon partisanship, and not on logic or law.

To that extent, the Republicans and Mr. Baker emerge unscathed because they were the ultimate victors in this matter. Nevertheless, I cannot emphasize how irresponsible it was for Mr. Baker to make some of his statements, such as condemning Mr. Gore for going to the courts in the first place, thereby implying that Mr. Gore has now resorted to "allow the courts to decide this election."

If the above is an accurate analysis as to the absolute right of Albert Gore to protect whatever legal rights he may have had in attempting to force a recount, then why did the Republicans' employ such strong rhetoric, and why were they so vehement in their attempt to sway the public opinion that what Mr. Gore was doing was incorrect, and that indeed the Democrats were attempting to steal the election?

I believe the answer to the above question lies in the fact that while Mr. Bush became the temporary winner by virtue of the original election results, he was far from being in anything but a very tenuous situation.

"Uneasy lies the head that wears the crown." Wise sayings have their place in our society. Mr. Bush was the leader after the election, but he could not rest and give up his vigil during the proceedings in the next five weeks. I believe it is safe to say that the reason American's heard such garbage coming from the mouths of the Republicans is that they were truly frightened that all of the jockeying and machinations of Mr. Gore were very close to accomplishing what Mr. Gore wanted them to accomplish; namely, a recount that would tip the slenderest of margins from Mr. Bush back into Mr. Gore's camp. The problem for Mr. Bush is what could he and his camp do but wear the crown that he was in jeopardy of losing? Could he, or should he also have campaigned for a recount? Obviously, not. Yet what is the only thing left for him to do other than to campaign for a non-recount, which is essentially what the talking heads of the Republican Party were encouraging when they made such statements as that of James Baker. It is always the more difficult position to advocate and push for nothing to be done, especially while around you there is a whirlpool of activity (by the Democrats) to cause something – anything – to happen.

There were several different ways in which recounts could have occurred with various segments of the votes. There were the absentee votes that had not even been counted yet, the military votes that were in dispute, the confusing votes where people allegedly thought they were voting for Al Gore and ended up voting for John Buchanan. Dimpled chads, those votes by the voting machine that had been partially indented, but not pushed all the way through to count as an actual vote, and other irregularities could strike pay dirt if a significant body of votes, for example, 20,000 votes or so in Miami Dade County were counted.

Therefore, the Republican camp did the right thing in doing only what they could do, essentially becoming a watchdog to the requests and demands through lawsuits of the Democrats. Wherever there was a lawsuit requesting something that the Republicans deemed was improper or hoped that the courts themselves would find improper, the Republicans brought this to the attention of the court. The Republicans presumably won on things that were improper and lost when whatever Mr. Gore was requesting was legally proper and, therefore, allowed.

Could it be that the Republicans felt that the recount process was unfair and that Mr. Gore should not have the right to exercise his legal rights? I find that preposterous. Just as I have delineated the roles of the chaser and the chasee, it remains that after the initial vote, each side had its pluses and minuses. The obvious plus of the Republican side was that Mr. Bush was the *de-facto* leader at that point in time. On the negative side was that Republicans had to endure pummeling by Mr. Gore in his efforts to overturn this situation. For the Democrats, it was the opposite. They were the losers in the election, but one could consider that they had sentimentality on their side in attempting to show to the country and indeed, the world that the true outcome of the democratic event was that they were the actual winners, and the democratic process was going to prove and vindicate them.

There are many corresponding situations in various areas of law and jurisprudence that create extremely unhappy participants to a law situation, yet are allowed to exist. The fact that they are allowed to exist is not necessarily aberration or an error by the courts. They are usually what is considered a necessary evil to make the democratic system work.

Take inmates on death row, for example. This is not an issue about whether one is pro or con about capital punishment. The fact is that even with the death penalty, when an inmate is confined on death row, he could literally be on death row for five to twenty years before his appeals and delays are exhausted. Could this possibly be a justifiable situation? Aside from "Justice not being served" by allowing the condemned to remain alive, the fact remains that it is costing the respective state tens of thousands of dollars each year to keep that inmate alive and in the prison system.

Therefore, while one does not hear any person extolling the virtues of the death penalty system, there is also no great hue and cry to alter it. The conclusion must be that it is just a sticky situation and that the system in place, while it may not be perfect, cannot be readily supplanted by any other obviously superior system.

We have the same situation with a close election. It does not happen very often, and there certainly are problems that are raised by a gigantic voting population coming down to such an even split that it might be impossible to determine who the actual winner is. However, there were certainly enough procedural and legal safeguards in place within the Florida legal system that addressed the situation, and the recount process was implemented. It also ultimately reached a conclusion. Again, you will not hear one Democrat suggest that the conclusion was fair, but the conclusion was reached. It did not create anarchy in the United States, and the issue was ultimately put to rest.

In conclusion, the war cry of the Republicans, as soon as this five-week political dance began, was that the Democrats were attempting to steal the election. I think nothing could be further from the truth, and I also think that it was total irresponsibility on the part of those people who spoke out, ostensibly on behalf of the Republican Party, to promulgate such a position. I found it amazing that there was not one national spokesperson for the Republicans (or, for that matter, for the Democrats) who was able to just state that the respective parties were doing the right thing, following the rules of law, and squeezing out every ounce of procedure they could to try to bolster their own positions.

The final irony is that the criticism of the Democrats' actions was unfounded can now be exemplified by the fact that after George Bush was declared the winner by the decision of the Supreme Court, the war cry of the Democrats became that *the Republicans* stole the election!

5

THE MILITARY VOTE

I have perhaps not masked my disdain at the criticism each camp endured in their attempts to protect their respective rights by seeking to either overturn the election on the part of Gore, or preserve the status quo on the part of Bush.

It is clear to me that not only did each candidate have virtually unlimited discretion to do whatever he thought was appropriate in this case, but also must be true because the limiting factor would be going into court and having the courts shoot down any proposal that either candidate might have concocted, had the court thought that the candidate was overstepping his bounds.

Another possible situation might be where one candidate might attempt to do something without first receiving the imprimatur of the court; but in that case, just as in any matter in our system of law in the United States, the opposing camp would then immediately go into court seeking an injunction, or any other legal remedy, to keep the first candidate in line.

To suggest anything less is completely irresponsible in my mind and smacks of such specious argument and reasoning as to render the party, in its attempt to curtail the legal and constitutional rights of the other party crude and irresponsible.

I believe the military vote falls squarely within this purview.

The military vote is cast under a different set of rules (such as not necessarily requiring each letter to go through the postal system if attempted to be mailed, etc.). Nevertheless, there was a SPECIFIC SET OF RULES that spelled out the procedure for how military personnel were to cast their votes, and more importantly, how to GET their ballots to each voter's respective home state. In this case, of course, the home state was Florida.

Can one realistically think that collecting the ballots of personnel, for example, sailors on the high seas, is such a new problem that procedures for getting a sailor's vote to Florida while he was serving mid-ocean had not been considered.

If some party had been out to sea for a four-month detail, could one still realistically say that casting a vote in the presidential election was not an anticipated problem? I am sure appropriate guidelines for all problems arising in getting the military votes to their appropriate home bases had already been well established and were easily put into place many years prior to the 2000 presidential election.

It is ridiculous and insulting to think that anything less than the "business as usual" type of voting and corresponding ability to get the military personnel's votes to Florida was anything but routine in this election.

If there had been unanticipated anomalies, perhaps they might have occurred by our military either being at war, or perhaps some segment of the military personnel being in some natural type catastrophe that seriously hampered the process of getting the votes to Florida. Of course, neither of the two above situations, or any situation of similar ilk, existed at the time of the vote.

If this is true, then the votes coming into Florida would be subject to the rules and laws already in place, having been long prescribed by legislative intent, statue, and previous precedent.

While it is true that either candidate, by dint of the myriad polls and analyses, could hypothesize that any body of votes—in this case, the military – might tend to favor one side or the other, this does not change the fact that it still was that the same "business as usual" procedures were followed by the Florida officials when processing the military votes. Accordingly, then, the only thing that happened after the recount rules were being established was that each and every facet of what could be a crucial factor in determining the viability of any single vote or block of votes was now taken into account by both camps.

As usual and logical, the camp that thought it would benefit from the military vote – in this case, the Bush camp – pressed to have the vote counted. All the Gore camp did was to say that the votes must be subject to whatever existing laws governed the acceptance of any military vote, because Democrats thought that the vote probably would be detrimental to the total count for Mr. Gore.

The fact remains that both sides only could pour rhetoric on the fire. In other words, neither side was instrumental in actually affecting the disposition of the military votes. The votes had to be counted and subjected to the existing rules of law. Because the Bush camp thought that the military vote would increase Bush's lead, they magnanimously said, "Aw, let's count all the votes and give full faith and credit to your military brethren, and let's honor them by counting each and every vote (regardless of how screwed up any block of votes might have been)." On the Gore side, they said, "Look, we love the military, but laws are laws and the votes have to be subject to existing law."

Therefore, the popular and feel-good line was the Bush one; what turned out to be the perceived abandonment of our military personnel was the Gore line. But again, in truth, both sides were just spouting rhetoric, and the ultimate vote would be counted by the existing laws regardless of the respective Republican and Democratic positions or urgings.

As usual, if there were to be any leeway in the existing laws, such as counting certain of the military vote that could not go through the Postmaster General because the internal military system did not necessarily demand that, then where there was a conflict of laws, the court would decide which would be the applicable law.

All this is just "business as usual" in determining what votes were going to count and which were not. Unfortunately, each camp could never separate itself from the rhetoric and the partisanship of attempting to push what it felt was to its advantage, regardless of any clear, logical analysis of the situation in applying what would ultimately be the rule of law that determined which military votes would count and which would not.

It seems that virtually everything that was put into question during the recount was just a variation on the same theme. That is, each side seized whatever advantage, either real or by propaganda, that it thought would benefit itself and it clung to and promulgated that position to the detriment of what was both logical and fair. The fact of the matter is that both sides had made an original assessment that the public at large was to be snowed or given no credit for intelligence, and that at no time would either candidate be governed by what was the right and proper thing dictated by law. Rather, each candidate chose the low road and the propagandized view and said whatever he felt would garner public sympathy, irrespective of the governing laws in place.

Obviously, the final outcome was that the military vote was counted within the context of the existing laws.

6

THE CONCESSION

Howie Carr, a Boston talk show host and columnist, commented on an article that he had read in the national news. Mr. Carr was now picking up on the fact that Mr. Gore conceded the election, and then hastily effectuated a retreat, calling back the Bush camp and letting Bush know that he was withdrawing his concession because the election was simply too close to call.

Indeed, whether you agree with the tactics of Mr. Gore or not, few can deny that the election was close enough to warrant a second look at certain votes that heretofore had been included, or excluded, certainly merited a second look.

The local and national commentators who commented on the election, thereby commenting on the actions of the respective parties, now jumped on the bandwagon to lament how, in future elections, the concession process would be forever tainted.

They hypothesized that the losing candidate would now never concede and always ask for a recount, thereby stalling the essence of perfectly normal and acceptable election results. As usual, this point of view reeks of specious reasoning as well as a downright perverted rationale of what actually happened.

It is true that the concession is a useful and time-honored tradition. The losing party, seeing that loss is inevitable, graciously concedes, thus expediting matters and allowing everybody to go to bed early and have an easy night's sleep. However, when there is a close election, the concession is not the proper tool to use. Further, we should not forget that the concession itself is not legally binding. In other words, a candidate who concedes, such as Mr. Gore, has not done anything of a legal nature, thus forever forfeiting the election or any chance that he might have to resurrect his own chances of winning the election.

I suspect that Howie Carr in Boston, was speaking tongue in cheek when he outlined how the concession would now forever prolong politics and elections and not allow the winner his rightful place on election eve. Nevertheless, even things said in jest, have an insidious ring of truth. I did not read the national news article, but there seems definitely to have been both a mean-spiritedness, poor reasoning, and a partisan bent connected in Howie Carr's column.

I would not be too far out of line to suggest that Mr. Carr is a Republican, and like virtually every person who commented on the election results themselves, he could not keep the actual facts and logical reasoning from intertwining his own political beliefs and voicing an opinion that was partisan.

Of course, a candidate cannot arbitrarily always demand a recount, irrespective of the actual results. There has to be a semblance of closeness, and saner heads will prevail on deciding whether the closeness of the election itself does warrant a recount. Existing laws or certainly going into court to get appropriate restraining orders to stop a frivolous recount would always be available to the victorious party. Again, as is the common theme in this book, there was no single aspect of the post election results that was not or could not be commented upon, acted upon, and analyzed without the partisan twist permeating whatever was being talked about or analyzed. The concession was no different.

7

THE REVOTE

What was never seriously discussed nor ever seriously considered was having the whole state of Florida have another vote to determine whether Mr. Gore or Mr. Bush should be the absolute vote getter.

Now, some might say that implementing a second vote would go against all tenets of democracy; it clearly was not allowed in the laws, or legislative intent, or any other conceivable legal directive. This is probably true. However, this does not mean that a revote could not have been implemented.

We revert to the old standby of running back into court. Either party could have petitioned the court for a recount. While the judges could listen to the arguments and analyze previous cases, examine the law and especially the legislative intent, and conclude that there was no leeway to consider such a revote, the fact remains that the courts still had the power to order such a new vote. The court could essentially do whatever it wanted, subject, of course, to further absolute review. If, as Supreme Court Justice Stevens hypothesized, "we may truly never know who the actual majority vote getter was in Florida," then it would seem almost that there would have to be a new vote because no winner was actually determined!

Like everything else, there would have been one camp much more in favor of a new election than the other camp. In evaluating who would have wanted a new vote more, Mr. Bush always had the luxury of being in the lead, so it would not make much sense for him to espouse any type of total revote. How could that make sense for the Bush camp where he was the winner at that point in time, and all he could do would be to become the loser? There are two responses to this. On the one hand, he could have wanted a revote because he might have considered that the sum of all the actions, especially the legal actions that the Democrats were pushing for might have been actually implemented, where the more favorable actions that the Bush side were advocating (such as no recounts) would not have been allowed. Rather than rely on such a selective process, the Bush camp may have concluded that a controlled total revote might be best. However, Mr. Bush no doubt chose the more logical choice of remaining the frontrunner and letting Mr. Gore do the chasing.

As I have said several times because the actual results are that Mr. Bush prevailed, what ever he did at any point in time can never be criticized, because the ultimate goal was to win the election, which Mr. Bush did!

It is perhaps unfortunate that each side could not have been evaluated and graded separately on each distinctive and important issue that came up, but the ultimate tally falls to the age-old finding of there being a winner and a loser. Everybody remembers the winner, nobody remembers the person who came in second.

The arguments to support the contention that there should be no second vote are many. People could suggest fraud and coercion, or they could suggest that the same parties who voted for one candidate might very well change their minds the second time around.

With respect to the fraud argument, that really did not come into play, because there was no fraud or irregularities alleged the first time, and no allegations (except some very minimal complaints that the

Republicans were getting a little too vocal) of any strong-arm tactics or anything else not according to law. Therefore realistically, I do not think that would have been a problem in a second vote.

The second argument would be that perhaps a second vote is unprecedented in American history and just was not right. In other words, the people voted and their voices were heard the first time around, and that should be what determined the vote. The problem with this is that it was conceded by many people on both sides of the issue that we may never truly know who was the winner of the Florida popular vote. This is so because, taking all the irregularities in to account, one could probably go crazy trying to assess whether one irregularity in Bush's favor offset another irregularity in favor of Gore. For instance, it was alleged that parties who thought they were voting for Gore ended up voting for Buchanan. We then had many votes in Miami-Dade County that were uncounted, and it was thought that these votes would significantly tip the scales of the absolute vote, most likely for Mr. Gore. Any such statement is always made by supposedly analyzing the make up of the county from which the votes came. For that matter, even the military votes could be significantly changed, because the military would have the right and the opportunity to recast their votes, and I am sure the military would have taken great pains to have all votes cast in a proper, legal manner and delivered in a timely fashion to authorities in Florida. The prevailing thought on military votes was that the military tended to side with Mr. Bush.

The argument that parties might just change their opinions in the usual course of events also will not hold up. This is so because in analyzing this, there is nothing wrong with the fact that perhaps parties would change their votes voluntarily. First of all, there is the argument that the crossover votes would probably equal out. Second, if indeed the crossover votes significantly favored one candidate over the other, so be it. After all, the vote was an attempt to establish how the majority felt about the candidates. While perhaps the original vote was to be how the majority felt about the candidates on November 7, 2000, it would not have been unthinkable that another vote would have determined the majority feeling circa December 15, 2000.

If all of the above arguments can be sufficiently argued against why it would not have been such a bad thing to have a second vote, why was a second vote not seriously considered as much as everything else during the five weeks of turmoil.

I believe the answer very simply is found in two words: Nader and Buchanan (as well as any other independent parties running for President). In other words, no matter how much one might try, one can never change the fact that the number of voters changing allegiance from Gore to Bush or vice versa, may have been insignificant, there would be voters who chose Mr. Nader, Mr. Buchanan, or some other candidate the first time could not be sufficiently monitored.

With a new vote, a Buchanan or Nader supporter would be allowed to revote and cast his or her ballot for either Mr. Gore or Mr. Bush, given the fact that it would be pointless to vote for Mr. Nader or Mr. Buchanan (the time for protest voting is over!)

This is different then every other argument I have stated. The reason that this is different is that the Florida vote, as any vote, was to determine a majority opinion of the voters. This majority opinion had to be made up of the collective opinions of all the voters of Florida. One way of determining a vote or a winner is in a negative way. In other words, a person or a candidate may emerge victorious because he garnered a certain amount of votes, but his opponent had to split votes with another candidate with whom voters identified ideologically and, felt that this third party candidate was a more attractive candidate.

There is little seriously considered dispute that most people who voted for Nader have enough Democratic ties and leanings that if Nader had not been on the ballot, they probably would have voted for Gore, either because that was their political leaning, or perhaps feeling that was the closest candidate to their ideology. The same thing might have occurred with Buchanan backers in favor of the Republican ideology: however, Buchanan did, in fact, receive significantly fewer votes than Mr. Nader did.

Therefore, I suggest that based mostly on the existing laws, while there might have been an almost insurmountable number of reasons that a re-vote would not have been allowed, I believe the most significant factor is this point: it would not have been fair to allow a second vote where there were more than two candidates originally on the ballot. This would have been a completely unmanageable situation, and the original third party voters could not have been monitored or otherwise sequestered and have their votes not counted. (In other words, allowing the state of Florida to vote again, but having all Nader and Buchanan voters promise not to vote a second time.)

Therefore, I think that is why the issue of a revote did not get much press.

8

THE RECOUNT

I think the word "recount" is a bit of a misnomer. I say this because what Mr. Gore was trying to get was not so much a recount as it was a re-evaluation of all the existing votes and the problems that might have been encountered with the various votes while they were being counted.

In other words, in times past, when there were no sophisticated voting machines, and when we did not have the technology of the year 2000, I believe the recount did connote the votes in question being laboriously and meticulously recounted. If the voting had been done by hand, and the corresponding count of the votes had been done by hand, then one could see that a true recount might have been accomplished. In other words, what one might have been faced with would be a whole pile of votes, all hand cast, and just in a jumble, perhaps in bundles with wire holding them together.

Without the back-up of a machine result where the votes would have been carefully put in piles, who is to say that the original vote counter might have become confused or otherwise mixed up a whole set of votes and put one set of votes in the other pile? Who is to say that one set of votes was erroneously miscounted, or counted twice? While I am sure it is possible that the same ills that could have contaminated the vote one hundred years ago might have contaminated this vote, I believe the likelihood of that is far less in the present day.

Also, there can always be the issues of fraud and coercion which if they existed, could have contaminated the vote. I suggest that any missteps like that might have been far more prevalent one hundred years ago than today. Indeed, with all the wrangling and posturing on both sides, let alone the occasional attempt at legitimate positions actually bolstered by law, that with precious little accusation of any fraud or any tampering or any other type of illegal activity that harkened back to the notorious strongholds of the past like Tammany Hall or the Daley stronghold in Chicago, then we have to conclude that the original count was a pretty accurate tally.

This being the case, then the actual recount by Mr. Gore was going to be less of a recount in the original sense of the word and more of an examination of the votes that were challenged or not counted for one reason or another. I think this is a significant concept and not to be tossed aside or trivialized. In other words, when votes were going to be re-examined to determine whether they were good votes that had been uncounted because of the "hanging chads," the votes were not so much being recounted as they were being re-evaluated.

Accordingly, I think the logical conclusion of this position is that Mr. Gore understood that a pure and simple "recount" was far more unlikely to significantly turn the tables on the absolute outcome of the tally of the votes. This must be considered logically true because we cannot forget the sheer number of the original votes, which tallied approximately six million. No person and, more importantly, no statistician would dare predict that if six million new votes were recast in Florida, the results would be precisely the same or even anywhere near the same. The count of the votes of this election was so accurate and so unlikely to be error-prone that recounting the votes as they existed would not realistically alter the amount of votes for each candidate by any significant margin. It had to be the specific challenges of certain votes in counties that, *en masse*, were not counted or not allowed for various irregularities, that would be the real hope of the Gore camp. Those votes were the only thing that could change the absolute vote.

Therefore, it was up to Al Gore to either recognize this fact and take the high (noble) road and act accordingly, at the much higher risk of not being able to overturn the results, or take the low road by obfuscating the situation in hopes that if enough confusion were created, just one set of the here-to-for discounted votes now would be counted (or, conversely, previously counted votes would now be excluded) that would significantly alter the total tally.

Although I do not necessarily condemn Mr. Gore for attempting to engage the more confusing and risky action, as indeed his course of action was, every other course of action upon which I have commented was easily governed by all the officials keeping their eyes on each other, but ultimately monitored by the courts. It seems that this was one of many situations about which each camp chose to not be forthright with the American public and to attempt to put its own spin on things in an attempt to gain the ultimate Advantage so preciously sought.

In other words, the recount was not a recount at all. The post election process of trying to get a total tally of the votes cast in the November 7th election was really an evaluation and re-evaluation of all the challenged votes: votes that had not been punched properly through the voting machine (chads); ballots that had been almost punched through but not enough to be counted as a vote the first time around (hanging chads); whether the butterfly ballots in certain counties were confusing enough to substantially render the ballots, as they were, improper or unconstitutional and thereby mandate a further election proceeding and the 20,000 or so ballots that were not counted due to irregularities in Miami Dade County.

Therefore, as the reader can see, officials overseeing the post election process had their hands full with trying to address all these irregularities rather than really challenging the machine counts of all the votes that had been essentially counted and tallied correctly. That is why I state that the recount is really a misnomer, and that it was really the aggregate actions of addressing all the irregularly cast ballots that would be the real focal point of the post election proceedings.

If one views the "recount" in this manner, then the reader can appreciate why the Bush camp had to be on their highest vigil. If the recount was only going to be a verification of the same votes that had been properly counted in the first place, there was virtually no chance of having enough change in the votes to actually turn around even the original 573 votes that were the winning margin of Mr. Bush. These specific situations were spread across the state and merited the attention and vigilance of the bush camp to keep Mr. Gore's assertions and attempts to re-evaluate these votes from coming to fruition.

Realistically, Mr. Gore would only be able to change the election if he could attack a pocket of votes that were in dispute rather than actually recounting the votes, which means essentially recounting the good votes that were done properly by machine.

One could always say that any re-evaluation of a set of disputed votes could also go in favor of Mr. Bush. This did in fact happen with the military vote.

Therefore, viewing the recount in this manner, it actually is surprising that with all the urgings of the Gore camp, that one pocket of disputed votes did not come in to significantly tip back the popular vote to Mr. Gore's side.

9

DISENFRANCHISED

One of the main arrows in Mr. Gore's quiver of legal theory in his quest for the Presidency was the fact that certain votes were not counted in certain counties. The natural follow up to this concept was to attempt to convince the powers that be – in this case, the courts – that certain parties as a group would be disenfranchised if their votes were not counted.

The attorneys representing the Gore camp uttered eloquent pleas about how much of a travesty it would be if certain groups of votes were not given their due. These lawyers became the champions to those anonymous voters. They vehemently and passionately plead for the rights of the voters who would be disenfranchised if the total votes for certain counties were not counted. In this case, some votes were counted, and portions of the votes were excluded for various reasons.

Being what it is, the nature of politics sometimes constrains the candidates from simply stating what they mean and asking for what they want. God forbid that Mr. Gore would have said the day after the election that of course he wanted to be the President of the United States. In fact, he probably wanted that more than anything else he had ever wanted in his life. This is not to say that he did not also have obligations to try to serve the mandate of the people of his party and become the President (assuming that he actually received the majority of votes within the confines and rules of how a majority was determined).

Nevertheless, such a forthright statement did not come from Mr. Gore. Mr. Bush was in the same position although all pronouncements and opinions against him are always blunted by the fact that he became the leader in the election by dint of the fact that both the initial and the subsequent official count of the Florida votes, not counting the myriad of disputed votes, came out in his favor.

Therefore, we had the rather anomalous situation that the Gore attorneys were fervently pleading for the rights of these unnamed and unaccounted voters, passionately stating that their rights would be violated if in fact the court did not allow their votes to be counted.

I suggest that the Gore camp's attempt to so diligently protect the rights of these voters was quite misplaced on the one hand (but of course this is irrelevant because they had to argue for the rights of those voters because their goal was to make something – anything – happen to have these extraneous votes counted.) I believe that the Bush team missed the most cogent and logical of arguments in its attempt to stop these votes from being counted. What I suggest, and some might find this rather radical, is that the bush team was reluctant to utilize the following argument for fear of alienating the American public. Nevertheless, I think the following argument is much more cogent and logical way to label these types of votes and put these uncounted votes in their proper place.

The simple political argument, of course, is that every American citizen over the age of 18 has the right to vote, but more compelling is that each person has the right to have his or her vote counted. To not count these votes would be tantamount to trammeling on these unnamed voters' Constitutional rights. The patriotic rhetoric could go even further and say that it is the cornerstone of a Democratic society, and certainly the cornerstone of America, that each and every person has the right to have his or her vote counted, and to not count these votes would be the most terrible violation voters' rights.

I do concur that to have these voters, as indeed, all voters of Florida, the right to vote is in fact their basic Constitutional and American right to do so. However, the definition of the word disenfranchised is "to deprive one of the right to vote." Again, I believe that to systematically exclude a class of people for any reason, be it ethnic, racial, religious, or economic grounds, due to physical handicap, or to any reason short of incompetence, would indeed have been the most inimical thing that could have happened to any set of voters. In fact, I even agree that to deny any voters the right to vote would have been a serious undermining of a foundation of the American Democracy.

But in point of fact, the issue here is not that anybody was "deprived of the right to vote," as is precise definition of disenfranchise. What happened here, plain and simple, is that votes, were not counted for various specific reasons *after* they had been cast.

In other words, we must carefully examine what set of votes we are talking about, and determine not only why they were not counted, but ask ourselves about the origin of the votes we are talking about, and in this case whether it was by county, represent such a specific and identifiable segment of the population, that to suggest that they would not be counted would be tantamount to blatant discrimination. For instance, if one county in Florida were pinpointed as being 90% Jewish, and all the votes or even most of the votes of this county were somehow mysteriously deemed to be unfit to be allowed to be counted, and the situation was that this was the most heavily populated Jewish county, then at least eyebrows could be raised as to why the votes were not being counted. If such a county were in the limelight, the authorities who made such a decision would be carefully scrutinized to see if the decision itself had been made on an objective basis, free of all type of bias or partisanship. However, the counties in which the votes were in question were not so overwhelming identifiable with a party affiliation that they represented any type of statistical anomaly. Accordingly, in going back to the definition of disenfranchised, a main Constitutional safeguard was accomplished; namely, that all parties were allowed to vote.

After the fact, because some votes were now deemed to be cast either illegibly or in some other defective way, these votes were now not being used. These votes now lost their specific identity and could not be attributed to any specific parties, but for the fact of which county from which they came. This sole identification of the votes can hardly be said to be significant or being able to undeniably align them with a specific group of people or a specific party affiliation, notwithstanding the fact that the county itself might have been able to have been deemed either Republican or Democratic.

Therefore, I conclude that the impassioned pleas of the Gore camp were specious. They were ostensibly trying to protect the rights of voters who were essentially unidentifiable.

These voters were neither officially or systematically denied the right to vote. And after the fact, the votes themselves were not so overwhelming all encompassing (they only represented a portion of the votes cast in their respective counties), these specific votes could not be aligned to any specific political party other than the general classification of "voters."

Certainly, it could be said that the voters as a general proposition, should be protected. I do not believe this concept is being violated by singling out votes that were improperly cast and characterizing and classifying them as votes that should not be counted. The point is that while there is no reason not to count all votes if they are proper, the fact that some votes will not be counted if they were deemed to be improper cannot be specifically relayed back to aligning these votes with specific parties. If there is not such a one-sided connection between a party casting a vote and the votes themselves cannot be easily identifiable and highly correlated to the way the majority would have voted, (i.e., a county that may have been 90% African American who voted Democratic), then anybody attempting to bring a class action suit (which is essentially what the Gore camp was doing) but was really only doing it to further Mr. Gore's objective. This objective was specifically trying to create a right to a recount for the specific purpose of tipping the vote count to the Gore camp. The Gore camp should not be afforded the benefit of the doubt that their actions were only being done to "protect the rights of these unnamed voters." The only true and logical assessment is that the Gore camp was attempting to style an argument, any argument, to accomplish its ultimate goal of "mixing things up" in any way that would change the outcome of the election. The protection of those unnamed voters was one of the Gore camp's most fruitful areas of misdirection.

Does this mean that the Gore camp and the attorneys should not have used these arguments. Of course not! The beauty of the American system is that Gore's followers were allowed to use whatever arguments they chose. If they could convince or cajole the court that the arguments make sense, all the more power to them. The American system of justice not only allows this, but in many instances encourages it. On the other hand, if the justices had been more clear thinking and if the Gore and Bush camps had had the courage of their convictions and used this argument, they might have said that if a voter has the *opportunity* to vote, then subsequent improprieties do not render those voters to be disenfranchised. This would have been a far more compelling and much clearer argument in giving the justices the foundation that they needed to deny the Gore position.

Again, it will be emphasized countless times in this book, that Bush cannot be criticized for not doing something. He did win the election! In retrospect, not espousing this argument becomes rather trivial, given the fact that no matter what he did, he survived the recount and accomplished his ultimate goal and being named President elect.

It is a tribute to political posturing that candidates in certain situations will shy away from speaking (or stating) the truth because of the apparent impact it will have upon their constituents, regardless of whether the statements are true or not. I can only surmise that the Bush camp was afraid to stand in front of the justices and suggest that the votes already cast by this unnamed group of voters should not have secondary standing and power to be counted to "protect the voting rights of these parties," when there is no clear directive for this to occur. The Gore team attempted to invoke Constitutional right, because the Constitutional demands were that the parties be allowed to vote, and this did occur. The Constitutional demands do not spillover to the fair and accurate administration of the votes once their votes are cast. Obviously, the handling of the votes must proceed accurately and fairly and without taint of fraud or bias and without coercion or any other negatives. However, such negatives were not suggested by the Bush camp, and therefore the Gore camp was allowed to argue and came very close – and in some instances, did – eventually cause recounts to occur.

However, I think that the better argument is that once the vote is cast, in the correct way or not, the constitutional mandate is satisfied. Thereafter, what is or is not done with the votes in each specific instance should be determined on the unique merits of each situation and not the broad brush of the voters' "Constitutional rights need to be preserved."

10

THE TEST OF DEMOCRACY

As the election challenge dragged on, it became increasingly obvious that there would be no simple solution, and more importantly, there was going to be no quick solution to this problem.

While non-Republicans may not have agreed with Mr. Gore's right to implement an exhaustive array of challenges, people immediately foresaw that Mr. Gore was certainly going to take advantage of whatever was available to him. Recounts would take time, the analysis of those votes rejected as being improper was going to take a much longer time, and time deadlines possibly governing the whole process (as actually did happen) that might be put in jeopardy. One deadline was December 12, when the slate of electors had to be certified by the state of Florida, and another deadline was December 18, when the electors had to be returned on the federal level.

Accordingly, after the first week or two of infighting, the pundits, perhaps in search of new material to hash over, began suggesting that the whole process, and especially the way it was being handled in the courts and otherwise, was making the United States the laughing stock of the world. And if we were not the laughing stock, at least the prestige and power and reputation of the United States was being seriously compromised by the inability of the United States to elect its own President.

Of course, as with practically every other situation where both sides have the right to comment, the Republicans referred to this situation and, lamented that the reputation and prestige of America was being impaired. It was the Republicans who harkened to this point of view because it was always their position, since they were the front-runners, and they were pressuring to put an end to the recount in any way they could.

I, on the other hand, feel that this whole incident was and is and will be a marvelous reflection and primer for decades if not centuries to come on the workings of a democracy and the ability of the United States to handle what admittedly was an extremely delicate and volatile situation.

The United States prides itself on being able to pass the reins of government from one faction to the next at periodic intervals with no bloodshed, no posturing, and virtually no violence. In that respect, we are the envy of the world. Other countries are now able to do this, but we are the strongest country in the world and we have been doing it constantly since 1792.

One could consider that the 2000 Presidential Election was the most serious challenge to the orderly transfer of power that our system had come up against since 1792. And frankly, for my money, it seems to have been resolved in an illustrious and amazingly efficient fashion!

Let us examine what happened here with other serious and somewhat comparable situations. Periodically, our country experiences strife and turmoil when a rather large segment of workers go on strike. When a strike occurs, not only is there tremendous bitterness and rancor, but there is correspondingly serious violence. Picket lines are set up. People on the picket lines may have been instructed to physically assault parties who attempt to cross the picket lines, and for that matter, independent parties are occasionally hired to attack the picketers. It is not uncommon for there to be significant bloodshed, and deaths occasionally happen.

While there were some modest murmuring of strong-arming in several of the counties in Florida, which I believe was done more for posturing sake than anything that realistically happened. There was no bloodshed nor was there violence of any type throughout the whole state of Florida. Yet as I have stated, the passions of the nation were aroused to an almost fever pitch, and virtually every educated person had a strong and almost definitive opinion about which side was the devil incarnate and why the other side was one step away from ruining the country.

Speaking of ruining the country, one of the reasons put forth why this matter should end was that it was delaying the orderly transfer of power to the new President elect and that the country would become so inextricably behind in its overall time table that orderly transfer would also wreak havoc by its very delay. This also seems to be utter nonsense. Anything that is man made as opposed to a natural disaster and controlled in this fashion can simply be altered by the same men who are making the rules. Who was going to be hurt? Was it going to be the Washington DC landlords that might have to forego one or two months' rent before the new set of politicians were ensconced in their new jobs? Would legislation be delayed, and even if it were, was that such a tragedy? No. Everything would simply be put in place several weeks or several months later than anticipated.

There certainly could have been serious consequences in the delay if there were no one in power to make important decisions within critical time constraints. Some such decisions might have been the participation of the American President in some international peace keeping or other globally significant situation; or perhaps some party slated for execution might lose his only chance for executive clemency, because no one was yet in charge.

But of course, no situation like this occurred either. Business went on as usual, first because there was a President in place, Mr. Clinton, and the duties of the new administration would not be assumed until January 20th. Therefore, from that point of view, this whole process actually had several more weeks of dilly-dallying, delaying, posturing, and fooling around before the appropriate president elect assumed the reins of office.

All in all, I cannot even conceive of any deleterious effect caused by the delay of not having an immediate President Elect declared on November 7th or November 8th, but on December 12, 2000.

On the other hand, who can deny that this situation aroused the passion of a nation and it gave fuel to political analysts, talk show hosts, radio hosts, and political columnists. This action certainly animated the country in a way seldom experienced in this day and age. The day-to-day wrangling kept everybody interested in seeing which way the balance of power would tilt considering the candidates' moves within the Florida courts.

There was a criticism that the United States was becoming the laughing stock of the world because it could not handle its own internal affairs. Again, I think this is not only the farthest thing from the truth, but it was actually the opposite. History will be the ultimate judge, but I believe that this was democracy's finest hour. We had no less than the most important office of the United States to be determined, and we had a situation that might only occur once in a thousand years, and the United States quite handsomely, in my opinion, dealt with it. The fact that it took a relatively large amount of time only reflects the corresponding difficulty of the problem at hand.

What other country can brag that its political system and its political history could match that of the United States. This incident was just a reaffirmation of the strength of the American Democracy.

And this must be true given the wildly passionate views of the people as a whole. The election certainly stirred up opinions equal to, and I dare to say exceeding, such significant issues as busing, abortion, or gun control. Even those issues spawn more violence than the election did; yet I believe the election dilemma was even far more prevalent in people's minds.

Not only did the country survive; we emerged with a president-elect within the rules and parameters of the original election. I believe that there could be a no more fitting testament to the American Democracy than these five weeks in November.

11

PARTISANSHIP

One of the main reasons that I felt it was necessary to write an analysis of the election, was that no commentator of any local or national media, as well as practically no person with even a semblance of an opinion, could either analyze the facts or give an objective appraisal of what was going on in this election without coming to a conclusion mired and tainted by their political leanings and persuasion.

As late as 10 o'clock on December 12th, I was watching Geraldo Rivera and several guest analysts (he had four or five) wail and bemoan the Supreme Court's finding when it obviously went against Mr. Gore. The hue and cry went up that it was the most terrible decision that they had experienced in their lifetimes bar none. These analysts, as well as all the other talking heads, whether at the local or national level, newspaper, talk show, or live forum who were able to get their two cents' worth in, only could give their partisan wail at every juncture.

However, analyzing partisanship is a bit tricky. The reason I say this is that in this election, every topic of any importance had the Republican view as well as the Democratic view. The problem is that very few views or decisions on issues that arose would be of a kind that made either the Republican or the Democratic view completely right or wrong. This situation is not dissimilar to the old saw, "even a broken clock is correct twice a day." In other words, as each issue came up, it was addressed, and each issue was attempted to be disposed of. The respective parties certainly had answers, but their answers were always indistinguishable from their party affiliation.

For instance, I believe that in many of the most perplexing and controversial issues of today, such as the death penalty, abortion, equal protection, and affirmative action, each side of the issue is closely associated with either Republicans or Democrats. Democrats, for the most part, are for pro choice, no death penalty, and affirmative action. On balance, Republicans adhere to the opposite side. In most of these significant issues, I am of the opinion that there actually is a "right" answer to the issue at hand.

For instance, I believe there is a definitive, logical answer to the question of whether the United States should have a death penalty.

Obviously, the reader does not care what my opinion is regarding the death penalty, and I am far too clever to tell you my view of what I think the definitive answer is. Nevertheless, I think that there is a definitive and correct position. However, this sort of all-knowing position is quite irrelevant. The point is that respective parties had strong opinions on the controversial issues concerning post election wranglings, and if one party was not going to have an open mind, then in most issues, there is enough substance to that issue to allow both parties enough of a foothold to argue that its position need not be abandoned.

Therefore, when we now analyze the respective opinions of pro-Republicans or pro-Democrats in response to an issue, and even though there is little question that the speaker 99% of the time would only be voicing the "party line," the problem is that depending on what the issue was, half of the time the party line is going to be "position" right.

Take the concession speech for example. The Republicans would like to say that Al Gore had conceded, and therefore he had no right to call back and say that he was withdrawing his concession. As I have suggested, that is complete hogwash. Therefore, I would venture to say that that issue did have a definitive answer and the answer was, in this case, that the concession could certainly be withdrawn.

In certain situations the Republicans wanted to stop the recount because the standards were not uniform I think that was a correct position, and it was certainly borne out by the ultimate Supreme Court decision.

Because I believe that the Democrats had every right to do what they did, namely demand recounts where they could, and essentially crusade for whatever they thought they could do to have votes either recounted, reconsidered, recast or evaluated in different light, the Democrats certainly could be allowed to do that. My point is that in every situation, to which I have made reference, I believe there was a correct position and an incorrect position (or at least a stronger side and a weak side). If the speaker was on the "right" side of the issue, regardless of whether his opinion was driven by partisanship or true analytical analysis, the speaker gets the credit for being on the right side of the issue, regardless of his underlying motives.

President Clinton's view on all of this, which he stated several times, was that he thought the process was working exceedingly well. Both parties were maneuvering and otherwise sending out waves of their soldiers to do whatever it took to secure each party's respective side.

As I've made it clear in this book, I happen to agree with this position. The Democrats did nothing wrong from a legal point of view. What Mr. Gore should or should not have done as time ran out, is the subject matter of a following chapter. I believe President Clinton came off miraculously well in his assessment of the situation. However, one cannot truly ascertain whether it was the sagacity of Mr. Clinton in making his pronouncement and opinion of the situation, or whether it was just his partisan viewpoint because he was attempting to back up and protect the actions of Mr. Gore in challenging the election. The point is President Clinton gets all the points for his point of view, because it was essentially a correct analysis of the situation, and not because of his powers of political reasoning. We will never know whether his opinion was driven to partisanship or if he was really insightful on this issue!

Fortunately (or unfortunately), one cannot keep a score card as to whether the pronouncement of a person was correct because that person was "uncommonly wise" or whether that particular person, entrenched in blind devotion to partisanship and total commitment to his or her own political viewpoints, just happened to be "on the right side" of that particular question. I think that when you attempt to keep a score card, if the actor is lucky enough to be giving an answer on the right side of the issue (as I perceive each question has a "correct" position), then you have to give credit to the person espousing the viewpoint. You just cannot just say, "Well he's got the right position but he's lucking into it because he's partisan and he was going to espouse that (or "say that any way") position, whether it was right or wrong." I dare say, I do think this is the case in many instances, but you have to give the devil his due.

Except for issues that are so overwhelmingly one-sided that one cannot realistically embrace the other side of the issue, the issue of partisanship is one of the most complicated ones to assess and deal with. We cannot escape the fact that the answers, or in this case the decisions of the courts, especially the Florida Supreme Court and the U.S. Supreme Court, were going to alleged to be on partisan lines and not on the true "issues."

I believe the Florida Court, partisan to the Democrats, succumbed to this evil. The U.S. Supreme Court perhaps rendered its decision upon partisan lines, or perhaps the five majority justices truly addressed the issue objectively. Since I believe the majority decision was both correct and correct in its reasoning, those Justices get my benefit of the doubt as making the "correct decision" regardless if they arrived there by objectivity or by partisanship.

That is why an analysis of partisanship is tricky!

12

THE OPPORTUNITY OF A LIFETIME

At certain times in our lives every one of us has had to make rather monumental decisions. Some of us have had to make more of those decisions than others.

Sometimes there was enough time to carefully weigh all the options in an attempt to make the best decision available from all the data.

Of course, in many other situations, decisions have been made in a snap second, or at least over a very short period of time and much more hurriedly than one would have liked to make such a monumental decision. And of course, these decisions also could affect the rest of one's life.

Obviously, Albert Gore was at that crossroads the minute after returns in the election came in. His window of decision time was at hand. Indeed it could have been measured in weeks and perhaps one could say it was measured by five weeks when Mr. Gore openly decided to concede the election to Mr. Bush. Nevertheless, the more realistic assessment was that Albert Gore had a sufficient number of days at any point in time (but commencing on November 7, 2000) to concede the election, throw in the towel, and back off graciously.

There was no question that had Mr. Gore chosen to do this at any time prior to the Supreme Court ruling of December 12th, there would have been that lingering question of whether he did the right thing, or whether he was precipitously foolish and silly to concede the matter with such high stakes involved. Of course, this is the very essence of making such a monumental decision. Choices have to be made, and the consequences are not clear at the time one's making the decision.

One could say that Albert Gore had the *chance* of a lifetime when he was nominated for the Presidency of the United States. I say this because precious few people in the United States have been in a position to win or assume the presidency, from the inception and formation of the country to the present. We are inaugurating only our forty-third President, and of course, we can include all the people who were the opponents of these Presidents each time a Presidents four-year term of office expired or a presidential election took place.

To get to that point in time is also no trifling accomplishment. Mr. Gore had been the Vice President of the United States for eight years. While obviously the stature of the Vice Presidency does not compare to that of the Presidency, the fact is that Albert Gore was one of the major players in the United States in terms of power, potential, recognition, and stature.

Therefore, after the nomination and during the campaign for the Presidency, one could say that Albert Gore had the chance of a lifetime to become what few people before him had become: namely, the President of the United States. However, after the election, a whole new set of parameters ruled the day. Mr. Gore had to make decisions almost on a daily basis as to whether to keep fighting for his objectively less than 50% chance of overturning the election or gracefully bow out. What person in this position, even if that person had only a realistically objective 5% chance to attain the Presidency, would not fight with his heart and soul to attempt to secure the election.

And of course, in spite of what the Republican pundits were saying in criticism of Mr. Gore prolonging the election, Mr. Gore had an equal obligation to his supporters and the Democratic Party to attempt to fulfill the mandate he received at the Democratic National convention. Obviously, of the approximately half the country that is Democratic, certainly did not elect a standard bearer so that he could wimp out at the first sign of adversity.

There were also pronouncements and specious reasoning in the calls for Mr. Gore to back off for "the good of the country." As a practical matter, there were no negatives in prolonging the election such as mundane issues as the cost of prolonging the election (which the United States government can easily afford) and other ill-conceived arguments as our face to the world, or the chaos that would occur by the delay in Washington. Therefore, there seemed to be little downside in Mr. Gore pursuing his options.

But is that really true? In retrospect, in which much of the judging of any situation takes place, and certainly hindsight will be rampant in this situation, one can only speculate whether Albert Gore did the right thing by forcing the issue through December 12, 2000.

Certainly, this must have been the most difficult decision of Al Gore's life. It is very hard to abandon one's position when one feels one is so close to grasping the brass ring. Examples of the situation abound. Perhaps the most famous recent example could be comparing this situation with President Clinton. When news broke out about the Monica Lewinsky scandal, to actually consider admitting any type of a dalliance seemed self-destructive and down right silly, from Mr. Clinton's point of view. To prove such accusations would be almost impossible. Obviously, Mr. Clinton made the decision that not only was this his personal matter, but there would be almost an impossible chance to prove the type of allegations that were attempting to link him up with Ms. Lewinsky.

History now tells us this was a gross miscalculation and President Clinton misjudged the fervor of the press and the relentlessness of his political enemies, who saw this as an opportunity to undermine him, and felt that no expenditure of time, energy, and monies was too great to accomplish this goal.

The point is that no matter how embarrassing an admission would have been at the outset, in retrospect, the consequences of such an admission now seem trivial compared to what actually befell Mr. Clinton. As this book is written, there is still a possibility that he will be pursued and indicted after he leaves office. Nevertheless, as was Mr. Gore, Mr. Clinton was faced with a choice of enormous proportions and decisions that he had to make in a relatively short period of time. While examining the outcome of such a fiasco in retrospect, where it seems so obvious that Mr. Clinton should have bitten the bullet at the time and acknowledged his mistake, it must seem as plausible at the time of Mr. Clinton's decision to go the other way and fight the problem because of the chance of a case being made against Mr. Clinton seemed so remote, or perhaps the consequences of the admission were seemingly too large to justify him an admission of guilt (or culpability, or responsibility) at that point of time. Nevertheless, these decisions that we are talking about have to be compared with the enormity of the consequences, should the decision be contrary to ones interests.

Therefore, as I have titled this chapter the "Opportunity of A Lifetime," what I am saying is that while Mr. Gore had the chance of a lifetime to become the President, Mr. Gore had the *opportunity* of a lifetime to make a decision that would have been so sage, so marvelous, so astute, so imbued with foresight and hubris, that the aftermath might very well have swept him into the White House in four years. But of course, he could not bring himself to do that. He could not bring himself to abdicate the chance that he seemed to still have, the chance that was so close and so within his grasp that he felt that he had to keep trying to win the Presidency.

I am not for one minute suggesting that the right course of action for Mr. Gore would have been to abandon the election after the Florida results came in. I certainly do not know. (Although one could say that as each day ticked away, the decision became easier to find.) And one can say that to wait four years is an awfully long time to sublimate one's hopes and desires in order to gain what *might* only be a positive position after the four years is up.

This is not to say that delaying decisions such as this come up routinely, but they do come up often enough, and parties making such decisions do elect to put off their goals for a relatively significant amount of time. Olympic athletes are constantly faced with a decision that entails a four-year waiting period. Mature young adults are willing to put off the start of their professional lives by going into the military, or even pursuing extra advanced degrees if they feel that those courses of action will best suit them in the end. Young marrieds routinely put off having families, often for much longer than the four-year period we are talking about.

It cannot really be assessed whether Al Gore did the right thing by pursuing the recount and his objection to the election to virtually the bitter end. Only he knows whether, even in retrospect, he still feels that he did the right thing, and only he knows whether his inner circle of advisors at some point had changed their position and were suggesting that he abandon the recount in order to fight another day.

It is certainly undetermined at this time whether Mr. Gore can rise from the ashes and be the Democratic frontrunner in 2004 for the "Presidential race."

However, what cannot be denied or ignored, in retrospect, is that Mr. Gore had a marvelous opportunity to gain the respect and admiration of the nation (at least from the Democrats, Moderates, and

Independents) if he had decided early on to walk away from the election and work toward his goals four years down the road.

13

THE FLORIDA SUPREME COURT

Battle lines were being drawn and most interested parties could see that there was a high likelihood that the skirmishes waged between the Republicans and Democrats about whether there should be a recount, how the recount should be conducted, and other associated issues, were just not able to be decided between the parties.

This could only mean that the relentless controversy of the election would culminate at the doorstep of the Florida Supreme Court.

When this became evident, it logically followed that there would be a comprehensive scrutiny of the make up of the Supreme Court. It was generally conceded that the appointees were, and therefore leaned toward, heavily Democratic ideals.

Again, this did not have to mean that the Court could not render a fair decision. However, if one accepts my rather basic analysis that this issue was so controversial, and so passionate, that virtually no informed voter, from the very least of the blue collar workers to the sophisticated "talking heads," could easily render their decisions free of partisanship, then perhaps the Florida Supreme Court would also not be able to render the requisite unbiased vote.

Unfortunately, I think that is what happened. The political leaning of the Court, being Democratic, was certainly sympathetic to Mr. Gore. However, what "the Court" had going for "it" as I have suggested, is the phenomenon that while there might be a partisanship judgment rendered, if one can either see or argue or convince the populous that there decision is the right one notwithstanding the fact that it may be partisan, then one has to get full credit for coming up with such a decision.

Keep in mind that the Florida decision came when there was still time to effectuate further counting. For that matter, if the whole process could survive scrutiny, than there would even be an argument that the process could exceed the 12th of December, indeed even exceed the 18th of December, and, who knows, perhaps run into the date of the inauguration itself.

It is unclear that the recounting of the votes at the stage that the Florida Supreme Court received all its data, was a logical choice and that decision that could be made. However, what I do find virtually short-sighted and ridiculous, is the fact that a decision was rendered by the Florida Supreme Court without the court having set uniform guidelines to address and pass muster on the constitutional issues of equal protection and due process, in the manner in which further vote counting would be conducted. If the Florida Supreme Court understood this issue, but felt that to address it properly would be fatal to Mr. Gore's quest, then perhaps the Florida Supreme Court knew what they were doing all along. I will address this issue in the chapter on Closure.

We are now talking about the Florida Supreme Court that got its material on December 1, 2000, and rendered its decision on December 8th, thirty days after this dynamic five-week period occurred. The Florida Supreme Court could have had its cake and eaten it, too. It could have rendered a decision that either a) was just in and of itself, or b) quite partisan, but so close to an acceptable analysis of the facts that it could have been rendered for the wrong reasons but still be essentially acceptable to the American public. Perhaps the greatest *faux pas* that occurred was that the court rendered the decision without tidying up the constitutional aspect of it. The decision to allow (or at least not effectively challenge) the recount to continue "without further challenge" not even an attempt to set standards (both time standards and ballot evaluations) doomed the Florida Supreme Court's actions.

This being the case, I suggest that the Florida Supreme Court had no one to blame but itself for its incredibly shortsighted decision.

14

THE SUPREME COURT

Some political players felt that the Supreme Court was not going to get involved in this controversy. In order to intercede in a situation such as this, the Supreme Court has to decide that a federal question is involved. A federal question is one that rises beyond the scope of the state courts. It had been speculated by David Boies, Chief Counsel for Mr. Gore, that the Supreme Court would never get involved.

Obviously, Mr. Boies was a little shortsighted in that analysis. From a realistic point of view, one could say, "How could not the Supreme Court get involved?"

Certainly, if the situation had been settled and rectified and the antagonists had been able to release their claws from one another the matter would have ended. There was a chance that the Florida Supreme Court could have rendered a decision that would have been acceptable to most or, in the alternative, not so rife with unconstitutionality, that it could not have been realistically challenged.

However, the bottom line is that this controversy will be considered one of the major controversies in recent political history, and the Supreme Court is there to address such a controversy of monumental proportions, and the Supreme Court was certainly not going to miss this opportunity.

Of course, the great fear that plagued every tribunal and entity with a chance to render any type of decision was that when and if this matter got to the Supreme Court, the decision would be rendered along partisan lines. This seemed to be the logical position to assume, because logically, for the matter to go to the Supreme Court, would have to have meant that the decision of the Florida Supreme Court had been so flawed that it needed further appellate review by the Supreme Court. And if the Florida Supreme Court's decision was going to be flawed, it most likely was going to be flawed because of partisanship. If that were the case, there was a high likelihood that the Florida Court would have been so partisan as to transcend logic in rendering a fair decision in correlation with the facts (which I believe is what happened). Not too many analysts missed a beat in thinking that the Supreme Court, regardless of the fact that it was the most august court of the land with only the highest moral and academic credentials, still would also be partisan and perhaps not render a vote true to the facts, but consistent with political bias. Of course, the analysis of the Supreme Court decision, after the fact would be that the Democrats felt the Supreme court decision was unfair and, indeed, truly partisan.

Perhaps it was. However, the analysis of the situation is not simple and lends itself to much deeper scrutiny. First, to digress, when we talk about partisanship, there is an obvious antidote. This antidote is that if we are so worried about partisanship, then prior to testing the waters of any given court, we should make more of an effort to win the underlying election that controls the appointments to the court. In other words, Presidents appoint people for the Supreme Court. It is true that appointments must be ratified by the Senate so that the appointment in and of itself is somewhat tempered and blunted in its extremism. Therefore, the solution is that the complaining political party is just going to have to win more elections!

Nevertheless, if there were such a hue and cry that all nine participants on the Supreme Court would be partisan and one of the parties were leading in the appointments (in this case, generally conceded to be the Republicans), then the great fear would be that any decision rendered would be rendered according to and in favor of the Republicans because of the partisanship, and not because of the facts.

It is easy to say that if one wants to be on the winning side, then one should win the election and therefore guarantee that one populates the court with one's picks. This reasoning is not only simplistic but also fallacious. Any prior elections were always being waged full out for the one political party to emerge victorious. Nevertheless, I am contrasting this situation with that of anarchy. In other words, it is when the country is in chaos (and when there is military rule or otherwise) when parties are being elected not by democratic means, but by force, that the population does not have its fair say in any manner. The fact that we are a functioning democracy only means in theory, the complainers, whoever they are, had their chance to rectify and remedy the problem of having bad picks on the Supreme Court by convincing the American public that their candidate and their respective party should have been elected. Therefore, the conclusion must be that if there is a partisan makeup to a court, such as suggesting the Supreme Court is leaning towards the conservative, it must be said that this is the ultimate will of the people, and therefore, there should be no complaints.

Getting back to the Supreme Court, it is no secret that the court is divided relatively predictably. It was generally conceded that there would be four liberal votes, three conservative votes, with two people considered "swing votes, but leaning towards the conservative side.

There then would be those people that say the Supreme Court vote came out exactly as predicted, five to four, with the three diehard Republicans, Justice Rehnquist, Justice Scolia, and Justice Thomas voting conservative, Justice Stevens, Justice Ginsburg, Justice Souder, and Justice Breyer voting Democratic, and Justice O'Connor and Justice

Kennedy being the swing votes. In the case of the monumental Supreme Court vote that ended the controversy, the Democrats said that the vote just simply came out completely partisan, relying on the swing votes to "vote the party line" rather than voting the way they felt the issue truly should be decided, notwithstanding politics.

As I have stated in a previous chapter, there is a problem in analyzing a partisan vote. I say this because when there are two sides to an issue, obviously one side is going to prevail. Furthermore, regardless of who thinks one side is the "correct"; one side will have to prevail as the more correct decision than the other side. That is not to say that a purely objective person can easily ascertain what the "correct" decision might have been. It is just to say that one side will emerge as more "right" than the other side.

From my point of view, the Justices had to do two things in making a decision that would be both judicious and keep the country together. They had to give some sort of a timetable for this whole process to end, and, secondarily, they had to embrace any issues that they thought were so blatant that they could be used as the foundation of a deciding factor, and rely on that "obvious" issue as the justification of their votes and decision. I do think they accomplished these two goals.

First, with respect to the time limit, I have taken the position, which I think is correct, that in launching into the five weeks of political turmoil after the election, both parties had every legal right to do whatever the law would allow to try to secure them the Presidency. However, this situation can and should go only so far. Certainly, the process should continue going forward so long as there continues to be some definite game plan. The process itself was in its fifth week of its game plan, and anyone could see that there was no cohesiveness that would carry the day for a unanimous consensus in the recounting of the votes.

If it has not become obvious to the reader, it is my opinion that allowing the counties to do everything from determining how to analyze the physical indentations on a ballot to actually trying to determine what a voter was thinking, and therefore render a countable vote in that vein, bordered on lunacy. I hypothesize in the next chapter that Mr. Gore had a chance to address this problem, that the Florida Supreme Court certainly had a chance to address this problem, especially where the problem seems to have become clearly crystallized, and finally that the U.S. Supreme Court not only had a chance to address this problem, but they actually and finally did!

The fact is that on the one hand, the combatants had a right to delay matters because they had a right to avail themselves of the courts and the available procedures and the laws to attempt to verify the integrity of the election. But it did seem that things began to go in circles, and to make sure that the Democracy of our country was not strained to its limit, an end needed to be put to the proceedings. While the Gore camp might not agree with the following premise, I think that deep in the hearts of most knowledgeable and intelligent people, this is a realistic analysis. At some point, one has to realize that the safeguarding of people's right (the Gore camp), having been allowed to challenge and attempt to do what was necessary to change the results, became secondary to the orderly declaration of a winner, even if it were done under less than ideal terms and circumstances.

I think the Supreme Court recognized this, and I believe they made their decision with this concept squarely in mind.

The Supreme Court's decision would have been all the more questionable and controversial if there had not been a valid point to address or a valid point that could logically, constitutionally, and realistically bolster its decision. I think what the Supreme Court espoused in their majority opinion, that being that the difference in allowing votes to be counted and evaluated violated equal protection and due process concepts, and, consequently, the Florida Supreme Court decisions had to be declared unconstitutional.

Therefore, I believe that the basis upon which the Supreme Court made its decision is a valid basis and therefore not subject to any serious attack to its credibility. As I have said, if the Supreme Court could render a decision in that manner, then it should be above reproach and above the taint of partisanship. I think this decision clearly fits those guidelines!

It is difficult to analyze and segregate and allege partisanship because the label of partisanship becomes diluted, and perhaps completely moot, when the decision, even if it were rendered along partisanship lines, actually is the right decision.

While there may exist a situation in which the judicial body making the decision lucks out because it is making a partisan decision that just happens to be the correct decision, one then can nevertheless not deny the judicial body its accolades, because no matter how one arrived at the decision, the decision is correct.

In other words, regardless of how or why a decision was made, and regardless of whether the decision maker blatantly rendered a partisan decision rather than a logical and clear cut decision correlating with the existing facts, that body must be given full credit for the decision regardless of how the actor came to make it. It is just too difficult in life to have it any other way.

However, I think another facet of the Supreme Court's involvement must be commented upon. I find the statement made by Justice Stevens to be completely misplaced, and I believe it would have been greatly detrimental to the country if the country had been listening. I think that by the time the Supreme Court decision was finally rendered, the steam had run out of this passion play and, for the most part, the populace was glad to see it over.

Nevertheless, I think the statement made by Justice Stevens that "while it may never be known who actually won the Florida vote, that the American population has been greatly damaged by the decision." I believe this opinion borders on the irresponsible. And I believe this is all the more so because it was rendered by arguably one of the most revered and respected judges in the nation. The statement (and underlying position) is flawed on three distinct grounds.

First, I think Justice Stevens was correct in saying we may never truly know who won the Florida election. That being the case, it clearly became a giant chess match with moves and counter-moves, strategy and counter-strategy. A win would be a brilliant coup, and at some point the ax must fall and the decision must be made (not unlike my concept of the lottery). Whoever was standing in the right spot at that time, much like musical chairs, would be declared the winner. Mr. Bush had a lead that proved to be insurmountable. However, given the fact that Justice Stevens recognized the impossibility of declaring with absolute certainty a winner (by vote count), he also should have reasoned that the corresponding integrity of trying to ascertain such a winner was also meaningless. This is not to say the integrity of the national election and the whole electoral process was flawed; it is just to say that because of circumstances beyond anybody's realistic control, the rules changed enough so that a winner was going to be determined by factors other than the popular vote. (Of course, the popular vote was the firm foundation upon which all this wrangling was based.) As long as everybody knows the rules of the game and abides by them, this would be satisfactory. Again, not the highest level of perfectness, but acceptable. Therefore, Justice Stevens should not have condemned this decision with the label of a catastrophe. If he, himself, saw the impossibility of determining the winner of the election by a true tallying of all the votes cast, then this Supreme Court decision could be considered as good as any, especially since it was attempted to be rooted with some sort of logic about the constitutionality of the vote. The situation probably was best left unsaid, as it does seem foolish to trumpet the inadequacies of the election, if indeed there were any. One has to look at the whole and not just sum of its parts. Whatever was happening in Florida was only a cog in the whole process that ultimately determined the winner. The winner could not have been ascertained if it were not for the input of all the other forty-nine states. Therefore, the whole Florida vote, in its way, was successful, even though it was not decided in the traditional manner. Justice Stevens should have recognized this and not made a statement that inferentially condemned the process.

Second, Justice Stevens was clearly condemning the partisan aspect of the decision of the Court. As I have suggested in this chapter, this is just plain wrong. So long as the actual decision was not so abhorrent, or not so at odds with the facts that were the underlying foundation of the decision, Justice Stevens should have accepted the nature of a partisan decision, as this becomes one of the tenets of the Democratic system. The partisanship here is not so evil that it should be roundly ostracized and made out to be an abomination. Justice Stevens becomes an integral part of the nine member body, and like it or not, one is judged by the company that he keeps. He also is part of the negative of being partisan, but only on the other side. He has to be bound, and he has to show support for the system. While one may show dislike by dissenting on any given decision, and indeed one's point of view is manifested by his contrary vote, this does not mean that a party should speak out in the way that Justice Stevens not only meant to, but did with all the venom and malice and condemnation of the partisan aspect of the decision. If Justice Stevens has a political affiliation to which he has been aligned for the many years that he has been in public life, then he must not and cannot denounce the decision itself as partisan, as his own dissent is as partisan as the Court's majority opinion. There can be no higher ground or logic for one to hang his hat on other than to accept the vote because the vote is coming from the U.S. Supreme Court, and therefore, It must be given its full "faith and credit" (to borrow a phrase from the U.S. Constitution) as a valid and acceptable decision.

Finally, as I have made it my position in this book, Justice Stevens should have remained mum and not criticized the vote in the way that he did for the very simple reason that I think he was on the wrong wide of what was the correct decision of this issue and his logic is quite fallible. I have said over an over again; the call for clear thinking people was easy. To allow the vote to go forward by allowing each county such unfettered discretion in determining the intent of the voters, the half-punched chads, and the temptation to thwart or alter a group of votes because certain voters may have been confused by the ballot all reflected a rather easy constitutional issue to decide. The majority was right, not because this was the partisan position, but this was truly the correct decision to make in light of the facts and in light of the previous Florida decision to allow the vote count to go forward with no standardized rules.

Sometimes in a law suit the issues are so close, and the arguments on each side so compelling, and the Justices involved so hard pressed to come to a valid and rational decision, if they can find any niche in which to fit their positions, and niche is strong enough to refute the other arguments, then invariably an appeals court will gravitate to that position, just to be on firm ground.

The recount without standards was basically flawed and unconstitutional. The majority of the Supreme Court, regardless of whether they made their decision while looking into a partisan mirror, or because they truly analyzed it correctly and maintained the corrected position, did the right thing by stopping the recount because of the unconstitutional manner in which the recount would proceed. Justice Stevens and the other dissenting justices should have recognized this, and made it a unanimous decision. Had they done this, the decision would have risen above the taint of partisanship and would have given finality and correctness and an implicit peace to the country. Unfortunately, the tradition and passion of partisanship was too strong and this issue too explosive to transcend its inherent controversies, and there was a split decision.

As a final word, one can now only marvel at the wisdom and sagacity of having an odd number of people on the Supreme Court, so that we can always obtain a majority opinion.

15

CLOSURE

At the beginning of the five-week period that became the Post Election Circus, the initial war cry voiced by the Republicans was that the Democrats were attempting to steal the election. As has been analyzed in this book, the stealing of the election manifested itself in several different ways. All of these ways manifested themselves in no more than Mr. Gore's attempt to legally protect his rights and interests as a candidate in the presidential election.

Nevertheless, one could hear the collective gasp of all Republicans as Mr. Gore availed himself of all legal strategies to which he was entitled in his attempt to reach his own goals.

This is not to say that Mr. Gore was the villain in attempting to utilize all of his legal rights in order to gain a victory in the presidential election. What it means is that the role of chaser fell to Mr. Gore not because he wanted it, and not because he was a decisive underdog in the Florida Election, but because the large roulette wheel of life spun around and the ball that determined who had the most votes in Florida landed in Mr. Bush's cubicle.

It should also be noted in the post election procedure, practically every action taken by each Candidate had a reciprocal action that added to the sum of its parts. While this statement is not terribly profound, it is exactly what happened.

What I mean is that depending on whether you were Mr. Gore or Mr. Bush, at every post-proceeding stage, you were obligated to take the action that was going to most benefit and preserve or create the outcome that you were seeking. As I previously stated, because Mr. Bush was already the leader, his most obvious overall strategy would be to maintain the status quo. Indeed, if Mr. Bush could ultimately maintain the status quo, he would be the new President, because no matter how statistically insignificant the vote in Florida was, it clearly anointed him the winner.

Therefore, it was left to Mr. Gore to be, for the most part, the aggressor in his attempt to change the results of the election. This makes sense because only an agitator could make things happen in order to turn around the election results and have a different person declared the winner, in this case, Mr. Gore.

Usually, when one makes a sweeping philosophical statement such as that each action in this matter had a reciprocal action by the other party, this type of broad generalization can be tossed off as mere rhetoric. However, in this case, I believe the actual actions of each camp proved this point to be true.

While I have stated that initially it was the Bush camp that vehemently, violently, and beseechingly accused the Gore camp of trying to steal the election, the fact remains that once the Supreme Court had made its decision, ultimately paving the way for Mr. Bush to be declared the winner, it was the Democrats' turn to vociferously decry the results and claim that it was the Republicans who, either through the brain trusts or the Bush inner-circle, or perhaps more invidiously, the partisan findings of the various courts and ultimately the final word, the Supreme Court, it was now Albert Gore who had been unjustly served by the whole process and, indeed, should have been the winner. The shoe was on the other foot, and the Democrats were now saying that the election was stolen from Gore by none other than the Republicans, previously the accusers and authors of the phrase "trying to steal the election."

It will be great fodder for the political analysts of the future to endlessly debate each side of the question, one side condemning the other's move or decision during the five-week period if they felt their side had been unfairly dealt with, or lauding the results, depending upon their perspective. However, I believe that there is a definitive answer in all of this. With that definitive answer, the respective parties can know that each camp had its own legitimate chance to either affect the outcome of the Florida vote or could have its prolonged day in court, and that each party took its best shot and that, after the fact, there now should be no recriminations that the Republicans stole the election or that George W. Bush should not and is not the rightful successor to the title of the Presidency.

In suggesting the following argument, I need to lay the foundation of two distinct concepts. The first concept is that of understanding what is meant by the constitutionality of a law. The second concept is how one is received in court.

Laws, for the most part, whether created by the legislature of each respective state or on the federal level, are created by the actions and interactions of the Senate and the House of Representatives of the United States. (A law or an interpretation of a law can also be created by the finding of a court of law in a lawsuit (a precedent), but this situation is irrelevant here).

A law may have its germination when a group of citizens approach their legislator to suggest that they would like a specific law passed, or a legislator or group of legislators can draft a law and submit the bill to the Legislature. The bill then goes through several stages and evaluations, and if it does pass all these pit stops, then the bill itself might be passed and become a law of the state. A similar course of action would occur with a federal law.

Every law is not necessarily a constitutional law. In other words, a concept is molded into an acceptable law. If the issue the law is intended to address is difficult the wording of the law will be drafted so that it will be fair and will accomplish the purpose for which it is intended. However, the law or the concept itself may not necessarily be constitutional. If the legislator is convinced that this law is necessary, he will attempt to push the law through regardless of whether it is "constitutional" or not. Remember, when we analyze a law for its constitutionality, we are deciding whether the law itself complies with the tenets the Constitution says are proper. If it does not comply, then the law will not be considered constitutional.

Further, it should be understood that any given law at any given point in time may or may not be constitutional. That is, when the law is proposed, it may not be clear whether the law is constitutional or not. In other words, the constitutionality of a law may very well have to be determined by a court of law at the appropriate level. In other words, if a law is challenged in a lawsuit, a trial judge is asked to determine whether it is constitutional or not. If a trial judge makes a decision and the losing side decides that the decision is wrong, then the whole decision gets appealed to the Appeals Court. There are a series of courts that keep increasing in stature until the law gets to the federal level, and indeed may even ultimately go to the Supreme Court of the United States. It should be realized that at each and every level, a decision is being made as to whether the particular law is constitutional or not constitutional. Even when one court decides on the constitutionality of the law, the very fact that it now gets appealed to the next highest court means that we still do not know if the law is constitutional or not. The court at each level always has precedence over the previous decisions. Only when there is a finality, either by the Supreme Court of the United States, or a lower court with no further appeals, can one say that a law has been deemed to be constitutional.

Also, the constitutionality of a law can actually change. In other words, by the climate of the country, and by the climate and make-up of any specific appeals courts, the same issue that had been definitively found to be constitutional in years past can now be declared to be unconstitutional. The rage about abortion is such an issue. Prior to *Roe v. Wade* in 1973, it was unconstitutional for a person to have an abortion. With appropriate guidelines, the Supreme Court in *Roe* now declared that in certain situations an abortion is the right of the female carrying the child. However, as most anybody understands today, there is quite a vocal minority (majority?) that would like *Roe v. Wade* to be overturned and to make abortion illegal again.

Therefore, the decision as to whether a certain law or situation is constitutional or unconstitutional is quite complex. Rather serious decisions can be made by either relying on the present existence of the constitutionality of a law, or even taking a more daring stand that the issue in question is unconstitutional (even when its issue appears to be protected by an existing law). The party taking the contrary stand will be vindicated by his anticipated lawsuit and challenge to the constitutionality of the law.

The second issue to understand before I get to the meat of my hypothesis is the interplay between parties and attorneys approaching the court decisions.

In certain legal situations, while you may have two parties obviously on opposite sides of the issue quite vehemently contesting a certain issue, the interplay and intervention of the court can be quite cut and dried and abrupt. What I mean by this is that while the parties themselves may be contesting either a law or a fact, when they get before a judge to plead their respective positions, they might find an unreceptive atmosphere with respect to the judge. This would occur if the judge takes the position that the fact or point of law being disputed is so clear on the law books, and the interpretation is such that there can be no ambiguity, that the judge has no leeway to entertain what one of the participants feels is a valid interpretation of the situation.

For instance, there might be a dispute about the ownership of property, and the document in contention would be a deed that clearly delineates that party A is transferring the deed to party B for a certain amount of money. Party A now comes forth and says that he did not understand the true value of the property, and he greatly undervalued the property, and therefore he virtually gave the property away to Party B. He is coming into court to ask the judge to agree with him and have the judge rescind the contract and restore the property back to Party A. However, in a fact pattern such as this, all Party B needs to say is that he was not confused about the terms of the contract and he knew that he was negotiating to purchase the piece of property for precisely the amount of money stated in the contract. While Party B recognized that he was getting a good value, he in no way felt that Party A did not understand what he was doing, and that Party A voluntarily entered into the contract under the precise terms that were reflected in the contract. In a situation such as this, I dare say that Party A would be met quite harshly by the trier of fact (the Judge) in that there would be actual verbal discussion in the court by the judge saying something like this to Party A "I can appreciate your position and I sympathize with the fact that you have now lost a valuable piece of property for an extremely low price. However, my hands are tied and I am forced to make a decision according to the written document, and I have no leeway but to find that the written document controls and that the transaction stands, and that Party B is now the true owner of that property."

However, while a lawsuit could very well go forward in the manner described above, there are a myriad of disputes and lawsuits that are not nearly as cut and dried. There may indeed be tremendous give-and-take in the courtroom between the parties and the judge, and it could very well be that the artfulness of one of the respective attorneys is the difference between one of the parties winning or losing his dispute. Most issues are not so cut and dried that the judge can easily cite one side as being absolutely correct, but each side could have fair arguments and logic to bolster its position (i.e., the abortion issue). There are far more of these gray area cases that make choices far more perplexing, and make the judge a bit uneasy in his absolute decision. A judge might have sympathy for both sides of the issue, but is forced to decide for one side or the other, with no compromise. These situations are more the rule than the exception.

Therefore, this now leads to a situation where the views of the judge, an interpretation of the facts, the artfulness of the lawyers' arguments, and many other subtle variables come into play in the outcome of a final decision.

Having said the above, now let me apply these concepts to what I believe happened in this election.

The first order of business is to hearken back to the initial results of the Florida election. While I have incessantly dwelled upon certain facts, such as the unfairness of the fact that Bush won by such a slight margin, and that whatever Bush won by was so statistically insignificant that it is not even recognized as the least bit significant in mathematical theory, the fact remains that there was winner and a loser in the election from the beginning and ultimately, the leader stood the test of time and weathered the challenges. Everybody knows that at the outset, George Bush won by approximately 170 votes, that figure went to 900 votes when the military votes were counted and allowed, and ultimately settled in the 500s which was the ultimate figure certified by Ms. Katherine Harris as the Secretary of State of Florida.

Regardless of all the philosophical, esoteric, lawful, and impassioned pleas and arguments of each side, there was no question that the initial results set the ground rules for the whole post election challenge. Simply put, Mr. Gore's party had to chase the election and Mr. Bush's party was leading.

Each party was faced with the respective mantels and titles that were bestowed upon it by the election results and was then free to make its own decisions as to what course it should take, what strategies should be employed, and how aggressive or reticent it should be in protecting its own rights. While it is true that Mr. Bush was awarded the name of leader by the election results, he clearly understood that this could be wrested away from him if the various tactics that Mr. Gore and his party employed – or tried to employ – were successful.

When the roles were spelled out by dint of the results of the election, each respective camp went to its brain trust, sat down, and mapped out a strategy as to what they should do. Obviously, the strategy mapped out was going to be, at least from each parties own point of view, the most beneficial and most intelligent strategy to utilize in order to gain the ultimate objective – to be named the winner of the election.

Being the frontrunner, Mr. Bush's strategy was one of reticence and passivity. He was not the aggressor for the most part. His strategy was to fend off and deflect whatever Mr. Gore threw at him, although it should be noted that Mr. Bush was not completely passive. He did bring several of his own lawsuits to have certain votes counted where he thought this would be most beneficial to his ultimate well-being. It only made sense to do whatever he could to reasonably *increase* his vote count.

The ultimate strategy upon which Mr. Bush settled may have been right or may have been very wrong. The fact of the matter is that the actual results stood up to allow Mr. Bush to assume the Presidency.

There may be those out there who vehemently decry the strategies employed by Mr. Bush. They may even say that the way he handled the post election procedure was absolute hogwash. However, whatever is said, especially if it speaks out against the strategy employed by Mr. Bush, is only speculation and conjecture. This is so because Mr. Bush became the ultimate winner. "You can't argue with success" is the only adage that reasonably summarizes Mr. Bush's strategies, because he

WON! The fact remains that you can love or hate the tactics Mr. Bush chose to use, but the true fact is that it is all irrelevant because Mr. Bush is now the President of the United States.

The reciprocal of this situation is the opposite of the analysis of Mr. Bush's strategy. That is, Mr. Gore had the same monumental decision to make when he entered the post election phase after the November 7 election. It should be noted that neither Mr. Bush nor Mr. Gore had to choose a blind strategy as they began their respective quests for ultimately winning the election. Both camps had experience and knowledge in situations such as this, and there have been many precedents over the last 200 years of the history of our country upon which the respective camps could rely.

Accordingly, the Gore camp was faced with the decision of how to effectively challenge the vote count that had been created on November 7, 2000. There were obviously several ways to go about this, and I believe we can hypothesize that the brain trust, the smartest people with which Gore had surrounded himself – and, indeed, I believe they must have been a savvy, knowledgeable, and intelligent group of people (after all we are talking about the Presidency of the United States) – to decide exactly what the best strategy would be to challenge certain voting totals where they had to, to attempt in other situations to try to have the uncounted votes counted when they assumed those votes would be beneficial for Mr. Gore, to try to eliminate the votes from other groups if the vote count would be detrimental to the totals for Mr. Gore, and, in general, to have an overall game plan so as to maximize their chances of reversing the vote count and having the majority vote count come out in favor of Mr. Gore.

Obviously, the above is just plain common sense, and of course there should be little question that the Gore team immediately began to converge, caucus, and strategize concerning the overall course that they would pursue.

Let us now examine that strategy. Obviously, Gore and his team were privy to the same information that became contested during the five weeks after the election. This information had to do with the voting machines, the indecisiveness of certain ballots, the partial punching or indentation of certain ballots, the more violently punched cards where in we learned the word "chad," and even the concept of a party being able to ascertain the intent of the voter by examining the voting patterns and the indentations of the voting card as a whole.

In formulating its game plan, the Gore team must have known certain facts. The existing law of the state of Florida was that each and every county was allowed to have its County Supervisor determine both the way votes would be recounted and evaluated. In other words, one can see that there is a wide divergence in the way contested ballots would be handled. A contested ballot could run the gamut from being thrown out due to the slightest irregularity with the ballot to the other end of the spectrum where the people in charge would closely evaluate the ballot and try to determine the voter's intent by examining the other patterns of voting on the ballot in question, even when the voter had not attempted to vote for the President!

I suggest that the Gore camp was quite cognizant of the obstacles before it with respect to the recounting and the handling of the ballots in question. This only makes sense that they would know. After all, what would they be doing if they were not learning every possible facet of what could occur or might occur.

I now throw into the fray my reference and explanation to the way laws are deemed to be constitutional or unconstitutional. One could say that there were two possibilities that occurred when the Gore team was planning its strategy for its recount of the election. The first scenario is that the Gore team knew and fully understood the procedure of how each county was going to handle its contested votes (all different and with no standards as the law is written that each county supervisor could determine the manner in which it would evaluate the votes) and that further THAT THE GORE TEAM KNEW OR SHOULD HAVE KNOWN THAT THE LAW AS IT WAS WRITTEN AND AS IT WOULD BE APPLIED WAS PROBABLY VERY CLOSE TO BEING UNCONSTITUTIONAL.

In other words, there can be only two possibilities. The first possibility is that the Gore team and nobody on it and no other consultants employed by the Gore team, and the fact that the Gore team must have been privy to the greatest minds in constitutional law in the country, could have anticipated that the standard to which the voting would be held might very well be unconstitutional. Or, the other and far more likely scenario that existed is that the Gore team recognized that when they got knee deep into hand-to-hand combat that it would follow that the Bush camp would challenge the way in which the ballots were going to be counted and object to the procedure as being unconstitutional.

Assuming we accept the premise that the Gore team must have certainly known that there was a chance, and probably a very good chance, that the process of recounting the votes would be put into issue, we must assume that the Gore team made a conscious decision to go out into the various counties, advocate and promulgate a recount, and promulgate this recount in the manner that existed and was proscribed by law at that time.

As I have tried to show in my analysis, it is very likely that on November 7, 8, and 9, in the year 2000, the manner in which votes were to be counted and recounted might very well be found to be unconstitutional. The Gore team cannot hang its hat on the fact that because at this critical point in time (November 8 and 9) the manner in which votes that were to be recounted had never been declared unconstitutional, they could rely on the laws of the recount process that were in place and assume there would be no subsequent challenge to these existing laws. The Gore team was reasonably expectant that if it continued in this manner, allowing for the great divergences and discrepancies in the recount, it would ultimately be faced with court challenges by the Bush team. The Gore team should have allowed for this contingency and taken a preliminary and pre-emptive course of action in an attempt to prevent this possible fatal course of events to terminate its quest for the Presidency.

If any Gore supporters choose to believe that because the laws were in place and the possibility of the unconstitutionality of the way in which the votes would be recounted would be raised was too obscure to be considered by the Gore team, then I suggest they are kidding themselves. While I myself am an attorney, although not a constitutional attorney, when I first heard that each county would be allowed to set its own standards in the recounting of the votes, my ears began to burn. I couldn't believe that such a wide divergence or such a low threshold standard would be allowed to be used in something that should by its very nature have a consistent and equal standard applied to every one of its counties and their respective recounts. This is so because the votes are certainly all cast identically in nature. Therefore, while it seems inconceivable that the laws have been promulgated in such a way that each county could dictate the rules of a recount (and not uniformly statewide), but the fact was that up to that time, the recount laws were never challenged and thus they were not found unconstitutional. However, this still does not mean that the Gore team had the right, expectation, or even hope that this wide divergence of setting standards would hold up under the very intense heat and scrutiny of a Presidential election.

Again, going back and analyzing the way in which a law is found to be unconstitutional, it is a fact that a law may very well be put on the books and remain there for many years unchallenged. Depending upon the seriousness of the law, or in a case such as this, depending upon whether these laws were actually used to determine some significant election, it may only mean that while the law itself is defective, and perhaps grossly so, because the application and interpretation of the law had never been realistically or importantly challenged, then correspondingly, there would have been no person to challenge the law and consequently, no challenge to the constitutionality of the law.

What then happened? I suggest that the Gore team very well knew and understood what laws were in place, what standards would be used for the recount, and the very real likelihood that these standards would be challenged by the Bush camp. If this hypothesis is true, then why did the Gore camp choose not to attempt to rectify this inherent (and known) defect?

Before I answer this question, I pose the question of whether there was a realistic way that this defect could have been rectified. I think the answer is a resounding yes! The Gore team could have gone to the supervisors of each respective county, sat them down and explained to them what was going to occur in the next several weeks. The Gore team could have emphasized the anticipated problem and suggested that the way to remove this as a possible problem would be to then and there set UNIFORM standards for a recount.

Remember, there are two constitutional issues in question! First, there is the question of uniformity – having all counties consider the votes by the same criteria (equal protection) – and second that the standards were logical and practical (due process). Again, standards chosen may have also raised a constitutional issue as to whether the standards applied were actually correct standards, or whether the standards themselves might very well have been unconstitutional. The Gore team should have used its not-so-insignificant brain power to decide what standards it should implement at that time, tell or force all the supervisors who were in control of the counties to use those standards (notwithstanding what laws were in place at the time), and attempt to make the standards comply with anticipated future constitutional challenges.

While the issue of creating what standards should actually have been implemented might be a little bit more difficult and a little less obvious to even the Gore camp (as to what to anticipate a court of law might deem adequate standards), the very least the Gore team could have done was to remove the first prong of the constitutional challenge, the dreaded equal protection challenge of having non-uniform vote evaluating standards in place, whatever the subsequent due process standards that might have been chosen.

Back to my original query. One may well ask oneself that if the above is true, then why did not the Gore team recognize this and attempt to nip this potential problem in the bud. I think there is also an answer for this question. Plain and simple, the actual recount in and of itself was not going to be an easy task for the non-leader, in this case Mr. Gore. We cannot forget that we were dealing with a body of votes that had already been counted, and probably counted quite effectively and accurately, by various voting and counting machines. While it is all well and good to decry the inaccuracies of the counting machines, and certainly challenge the non-counted votes, the fact remains that six million votes were cast, and by and large, all votes were counted (except the contested minority). While there may have been different voting patterns in different counties and in different parts of the state, one could conclude that the overall pattern of the voting was an equal distribution of the votes between Mr. Gore and Mr. Bush. Further, while one could say that an equal distribution of votes still might create a discrepancy large enough to tip the election back to Mr. Gore, I submit that the Gore camp knew and understood all of this, and I submit that on November 8 and November 9 of the year 2000, the Gore camp consciously chose not to upset the mechanism and laws espoused for a recount in the Florida system because THEY WERE AFRAID THAT IF THEY DID ATEMPT TO UNIFY AND STANDARDIZE THE RECOUNT PROCEDURE, THEY HAD LITTLE TO NO CHANCE OF TURNING AROUND THE VOTES, THUS TURNING AROUND THE ELECTION ON BEHALF OF MR. GORE.

To say it another way, right or wrong, the Gore camp was not willing to be legitimate, come forth, and state, "Let's have the most accurate and precise recount possible; let us eliminate discrepancies in the manner in which the votes are evaluated; let us eliminate the equal protection arguments that will be created if all votes are not counted the same, let us set such a high recount standard that we will satisfy due process arguments; and let us live or die with an accurate and constitutional and precise recount that will ultimately and fairly decide who received more votes in Florida."

I further suggest that if in fact the Gore team had decided upon this tack, they would have been much better received in the Florida courts and even in the U.S. Supreme Court.

This statement now is in conjunction with the second part of this chapter in which I explained the difference between going into court against something that is a hard and fast rule, or the other type of lawsuit in which there is much give and take to be had and a party might very well win a law suit by the oral arguments submitted to the court.

We live in a funny society where even at the highest levels one can receive "brownie points" for the way that they have acted. A person can commit murder, and then attempt to have his sentence appropriately lessened by having people of the community come in and state what a nice person this murderer is. This procedure is not lost or would not have been lost in the political suits that were brought before the Florida and U.S. Supreme Courts. Any judge, no matter what his political persuasion may have been, would have been hard pressed to summarily rule against the Gore camp if the Gore camp had stood up and said, "Look, we tried to go and have a recount that was uniform, Constitutional and free from all bias." If the talking heads that represented the Gore camp were doing that, I suggest that there were enough layers of courts that at some point the justices deciding the fate of any lawsuit would have had to have taken this into account. If a recount had been stopped because of time constraints or other perceived deficiencies, such as Constitutional constraints, the Judges would have been much more comfortable or, if there had been a Republican judge ruling on Mr. Gore's request, be forced to say, "You know, this Mr. Gore has done everything humanly possible to try to effectuate a real and legitimate and fair recount, and the court is going to give him the protection that he deserves because he has been trying to be so fair in this matter (no matter what my personal or partisan biases are to the contrary!) I suggest that the whole climate inside the courtroom would have been so pro Gore that, at the very least, Mr. Gore would have been able to get a recount of every set of votes that were in dispute.

One can even see by the final Supreme Court vote that it was a close 5 to 4 decision. While it has been decried that the decision itself was along partisan lines, it is acknowledged that there were at least one or two swing votes that could have very well varied from a strict party interpretation. Certainly, these swing votes would have been quite sympathetic to a Mr. Gore (or at least would have given appropriate lip service) who had bent over backwards to try to comply with the Constitutional issues that subsequently raised their ugly heads and ultimately laid low the Gore quest.

Even if Mr. Gore were unable to persuade a Republican person in charge of the recount in any county to react in a consistent manner that would remove any taint of unconstitutionality during the recount, at the very least Mr. Gore could have been able to say to the judge, "See, I tried, it is the Republicans who are afraid to be legitimate, and it is the Republicans who insist on adhering to a regimen that might ultimately be proven to be unconstitutional."

As I have suggested, if a convicted murder can actually gain benefit by having his priest or rabbi extol his virtues as a person, at the very least, a judge would have had to take heed of Mr. Gore, who was saying that he had bent over backwards to attempt to ensure the fairness of a recount.

If the above is true, why then did not the Gore team understand this, anticipate this, and attempt to do exactly what I am saying? I think there was also a very clear reason why they did not attempt to act in this manner: the Gore team felt that if it actually attempted to have recounted within the guidelines that I am suggesting, plainly and simply, Mr. Gore would not have won the recount. After all, we are losing track of the fact that both Gore and Bush went into the court, and after a decision had been handed down, the talking heads analyzed a decision as a win or loss for either camp. In analyzing the decisions this way, perhaps one loses sight of the fact that any win or loss in and of itself is not an absolute win or loss. It is only a stepping stone to implement what ultimately was the goal of each camp, a win in the final vote tally.

I do not think there can be one logical argument against this explanation as to what actually occurred in the Gore camp when they mapped out their strategy for trying to change the results of the voting in Florida. It is hard for me to believe that Constitutional Scholars of average intelligence could not foresee this, and certainly the supposed best minds in the nation could not have anticipated what in fact did happen in the courts and what was the ultimate downfall of Mr. Gore's attempt to have recounts that would, presumable, change the majority of votes to his favor. Again, for my money, the only reason the Gore camp did not act in this manner was that they might have thought, for whatever reason right or wrong, that if it attempted to effectuate the post election vote count in this way, it could not overturn the vote lead that Mr. Bush had, no matter how slight it was!

The final issue that has to be analyzed is the strategy Mr. Gore chose – and again, I suggest that this is a strategy that he consciously chose (and that being to just push for selected recounts with no overall unified strategy in the way that I have suggested). Was it the correct strategy, or was it a gross error in judgment? The fact of the matter is that the answer to this question is not nearly as clear as the fact that Mr. Gore should have handled the recount in the manner in which I have suggested.

On the one hand, one could say that Mr. Gore almost pulled it off. He went as far as losing by one vote, a 5 to 4 decision in the Supreme Court of the United States, with the Court itself supposedly stacked against him from a partisan point of view. If you listen to Justice Stevens, he himself is convinced that the recount should have gone forward and the High Court's decision itself was terrible, and a terrible blow to the nation.

Therefore, if you want to hang your hat on that aspect of the proceedings, you can always say that, well, Mr. Gore almost made it, he almost was able to get the recount on his terms, and he came oh so close to winning (at least the right to recount!).

However, right or wrong, that is not what happened. It is my position that Al Gore ultimately lost because he consciously chose to go the route that he did go, and did not take the higher road. If the Gore camp felt it had no chance of winning if it chose to travel the higher road, then so be it. It might have been up against an insurmountable object, and it did the best it could under the circumstances. I certainly cannot be sure of these decisions, but given my analysis, I suspect that what I have said is true: Namely, that Mr. Gore was constrained to handle the recount in the only manner that he felt he could, because otherwise he would have almost certainly lost. One cannot say whether Mr. Gore's analysis was necessarily right or wrong, but one has to say it was the course of action that he (or his camp) exclusively chose to implement.

If one can buy into the above argument, then it follows that no Gore supporter should be upset with the ultimate results. Mr. Gore took a calculated chance, made decisions that he felt he had to, and implemented those decisions in the way he handled the subsequent follow-up in the courts of Florida and the Supreme Court. Given the fact that the Gore camp had the ability to and should have attempted to obviate the inherent problems of equal protection and due process and the constitutionality of the recount, and he blatantly chose not to, either recognize nor address the problem, then you must say that Mr. Gore and his camp "had their shot" or "had their day in court". They were the architects of their own course of action.

If, of course, Gore had acted in the manner that I have suggested, and still received short shrift from the courts and the judges sitting, then one might very well have complained that Mr. Gore got a raw deal. However, not only is this gross speculation, but it is also irrelevant because Mr. Gore chose not to do this.

It is not everybody who can say that he had his own fate in his hands, and he chose to take a different path from what was the most legally correct way to proceed. In retrospect, one has to condemn the Gore strategy only because they ultimately lost. There is no question that if the shoe were on the other foot – if Mr. Bush lost – then there might very well have been tremendous recriminations as to what Mr. Bush should have done after the election and what he did do or did not do that sealed his downfall. Correspondingly, there would have been unbridled glee at the brilliant strategy Mr. Gore employed to turn around the election to his favor. Obviously, there was going to be a winner and loser.

Nevertheless, I submit that it was a unique situation wherein Mr. Gore had the ability to anticipate the problems that he was going to come up against in his quest for the Presidency, and he should have had the ability and the foresight to remove as many of the anticipated problems as possible. Had he done so, he might very well have been able to turn the tables, and if the votes had backed him up, he would have become the ultimate winner of the election. Mr. Gore chose not to approach the problem in this way and, therefore, not only Mr. Gore but each and every one of his followers cannot now complain that the election should have been Mr. Gore's, nor was the election was stolen by the Republicans!

In conclusion, I am stating that the Gore camp had within its grasp the ability to coordinate the whole post election scenario. It could have gone to the county supervisors, sat them down and told them in what manner they wanted the votes counted. At this juncture, the Gore camp had another pitfall where it could have done it right or wrong. First, by at least sitting every Supervisor down, they would have eliminated the argument of equal protection because at least the counting would have been done uniformly. If the Gore camp were wise enough to suggest a means of evaluating the votes that would also pass the due process constitutional argument, then it would have done the absolute most it could have done to attempt to secure a legitimate recount. Only insiders in the Gore camp know whether what I am saying is accurate or not. However, I suggest that to think anything less is being grossly naïve.

Had any of the Gore operatives encountered resistance by way of counties that had Republican supervisors, the Gore camp could then plead to the court that it did everything in its power to ensure uniformity (due process, and hopefully a legitimate course of recount, constitutionality) of the vote. Any Democratic judge to whom they pleaded their case would, of course, have been sympathetic to Gore, and even a Republican judge would have been hard pressed to dismiss the requests of the Gore lawsuit had Gore implemented the foundation that I am suggesting.

Can you not picture David Boies whining to a Republican judge that the Democrats did everything in their power to ensure an accurate and equal recount of the votes? He would have been able to further say it was the Republicans who threw a monkey wrench into the process (if in fact that is what would have happened), and now the Democrats should be given all due leeway in order to effectuate and conclude a valid recount, even if it exceeded the time limits and constraints that the Democrats were running up against.

Again, I do not mean to suggest that the Democrats did not fully take this whole scenario into account; if they did, they obviously rejected same. This is not to say further that the Democrats felt that if they went this route, they would have virtually no chance to overturn the results. That analysis might be very true also.

However, after the fact, because Mr. Gore in fact did not win, it is easy to say that the Democrats might as well have done it the right way, and who knows what would have happened?

Perhaps one could say that a part of the final consideration of what to do could have been governed by actually doing what was right, rather than by relying on confusion and obfuscation. Obviously, in the heat of battle, the Gore camp did not consider the niceties of being governed by what was right!

The conclusion is that no Democrat should lose any sleep or complain that he was robbed of the election because of the stopped recounts. If the Democrats chose not to approach the issue in the manner that I am suggesting, then they made a conscious decision to do it in the manner that I am suggesting, then they made a conscious decision to do it in the manner they chose, and all Democrats now have to live with the results that were ultimately generated by their actions.

16

SECOND CHANCE

In a previous chapter, I talked of Mr. Gore's opportunity of a lifetime. That opportunity was to bow out gracefully when Mr. Gore could ascertain there was little chance of overturning the election results. The best way for Mr. Gore to have acted would have been the most sagacious way by anticipating the constitutional problems of the recount, and trying to craft a recount that would satisfy the scrutiny of any appellate review. The second juncture, which was truly the opportunity of a lifetime, was to take a stand early in the game and forego any slim chance that he might have had to overturn the election, and become the wise and elder statesman of the United States. If he could have kept a relatively low profile for the next four years, he most likely would have been a shoe-in for the Presidency in 2004. All this is easier said than done. However, everybody at one time or another gets religion, and it would appear that Mr. Gore finally saw the "political" light when he did concede.

Mr. Gore's actions when conducting one of his final acts as Senate President and certifying the Electoral votes, was done in an admirable fashion. Reviews were unanimous that Mr. Gore was evenhanded and conducted the proceeding in a fair and nonpartisan manner.

Mr. Gore maintained order, ousted those who were out of order, (in this case black Democrats) and did not allow other objections (not properly posed), or otherwise let the people voice their views that were not in accordance with the rules of the senate.

Mr. Gore did not attempt to trade off the incredibly slim chance that one or two electors would change their votes, thus having Mr. Gore declared as the actual winner, and so this scenario was also given absolutely no breathing room by Mr. Gore.

Perhaps this one rather fine performance as one of his farewell acts will carry the day for Mr. Gore come 2004.

As I said at the beginning of the book, I was equally amazed at first by the rampant passion that was stirred up by most of the educated populace in America by the closeness of the situation in Florida, and after the fact, I am rather astounded at how soon the Supreme Court decision of December 12th was made, this issue ebbed from the consciousness of collective America.

Perhaps in this vein, the people of the United States will have a short memory for condemning the actions of what they felt Al Gore's relentless attempts to win the election and thus gain the Presidency, regardless of the objective evidence at hand, and perhaps to forgive the poison of self-indulgence and power that fueled Mr. Gore's misguided efforts to change the results of the election.

Mr. Gore at least recovered to the extent that he laid a good foundation by one of his last official acts in the Senate. Perhaps opportunity will allow him to build on that for the next three to three-and-a-half years until there is a new candidate needed for the 2004 election.

Time will tell.